Strategic Plan
in Local Govern

Managing Local Government Series

Financial Management in Local Government (second edition)
by David Rawlinson and Brian Tanner

Human Resource Management in Local Government (second edition)
by Alan Fowler

Performance Management in Local Government (second edition)
by Steve Rogers

Public Relations in Local Government
by David Walker

Renewing Public Management: an agenda for local governance
by Michael Clarke

Shaping Organisational Cultures in Local Government
by Janet Newman

Understanding the Management of Local Government: its special purposes, conditions and tasks (second edition) by John Stewart

Strategic Planning and Management in Local Government

Steve Leach and Chris Collinge

General Editors:
Michael Clarke and John Stewart

in association with the
Institute of Local Government Studies

PITMAN PUBLISHING
128 Long Acre, London WC2E 9AN
Tel: +44 (0)171 447 2000
Fax: +44 (0)171 240 5771

A Division of Pearson Professional Limited

First published in Great Britain in 1998

The right of Steve Leach and Chris Collinge to be identified as Authors
of this Work has been asserted by them in accordance
with the Copyright, Designs and Patents Act 1988

ISBN 0 273 62414 8

British Library Cataloguing in Publication Data
A CIP catalogue record for this book can be obtained from the British Library.

10 9 8 7 6 5 4 3 2 1

Typeset by Phoenix Photosetting, Chatham, Kent
Printed and bound in Great Britain by Redwood Books, Trowbridge, Wiltshire

The Publishers' policy is to use paper manufactured from sustainable forests.

Contents

Editors' foreword   vii

Introduction   ix

1 The essence of strategy   1

2 The current case for corporate strategy in local government   9

3 The dimensions of corporate strategy   17

4 The development of strategic planning and management   29

5 The organisational context of local authority strategies   42

6 The political context of strategic planning   54

7 Core values and mission statements   71

8 Strategic priorities and strategic visions   86

9 Corporate strategies and council budgets   105

10 Strategic management and organisational change   121

References   147

Index   151

Editors' foreword

This book is one of a series of management handbooks published by Pitman Publishing in association with the Institute of Local Government Studies in the School of Public Policy at the University of Birmingham. The series is designed to help those concerned with management in local government to meet the challenge of the late 1990s. It is based on the belief that no period has been so important for local authorities to have effective management, responsive to both citizen and customer.

The mid-1990s have brought reorganisation to local authorities in Scotland, Wales and parts of England. No local authority, however, can escape the need to keep under continuous review its political and managerial structures and processes. All councils are caught up in far-reaching changes. Some of these come from local determination and decision, others from central government policy and yet others from deeper changes in society. New problems, issues and opportunities demand from local governments a capacity to respond in new ways. They have to become closer to their local communities, their public and the wide range of institutions and organisations involved in the governance of localities; they need to find imaginative solutions to the ever more complex problems of public policy; they have to manage their resources to achieve value for money and value in the services they provide; and they have to achieve effective management in all their activities. These are formidable challenges for the managers – and the politicians – involved.

There are plenty of management books, but this series is distinct. Its starting point is the need for emphasis on developing effective management in local government, associated with the need to take account of the particular nature of local government. The series sets out to be succinct and to be useful in the practical day-to-day world as well as being designed to be used as a prompt to management improvement.

In no sense are we pretending that this or other books in the series will show a *single way* to manage the local authority. Management is not like that. Our intention is to explore ideas and questions in order to help fashion the most helpful and effective approach to the local situation. We believe that local authority politicians and managers should draw on as wide a range of experience as possible but that this should be set in the context of the special purposes, conditions and tasks of local government. We hope that this book contributes to that end.

Professor Michael Clarke, Head of School of Public Policy,
University of Birmingham

Professor John Stewart, Institute of Local Government Studies
in the School of Public Policy, University of Birmingham

Introduction

This book is about the growing importance of strategic choice in local authorities. We deliberately use the term 'strategic choice', because we wish to emphasise our view that 'informed choice' is the essence of an effective strategic approach, in local government as elsewhere. There are many 'big issues' facing all local authorities. Strategic choice is one way of responding to that agenda, as opposed to incrementalism, ad-hocracy, or 'seat of the pants' management.

The growing importance of strategic choice has been recognised in British local government. The past ten years or so have seen an increasing interest in, and proliferation of, corporate strategy documents. The titles given to such documents vary: 'strategic visions', 'mission statements', 'core values', 'corporate plans'. But all try to say something about the future direction of the authority: how it wants to operate and/or how it wishes to improve the quality of life within its area. Such documents provide the most tangible expression of the new commitment to a strategic approach, which is why we collected over 100 current examples to draw on and refer to when writing this book (for details *see* p.3 below).

However, the existence of a strategic plan does not in itself mean that an authority is making strategic choices. A good strategic plan will express, shape or inform strategic choice. But we are aware of strategic plans in which the choice element is difficult to identify, and in which the content is dominated by bland and incontestable statements. One important test of a genuine strategic choice is that it should be possible to imagine someone disagreeing with it! We are also aware of strategic documents which although they identify real choices, can often end up having little or no impact upon the operations of the authority.

Strategic choices may, of course, be made without the benefit of a strategic plan (although we would argue that a good strategic plan provides an invaluable input to strategic choice). Strategic management – the process whereby key decisions are made in response to problems impinging on the authority (or decisions are made about the implementation of strategic priorities) – can and does take place without the prior existence of a strategic plan. The essence of strategic management is the ability to identify the decisions which are important to the future of the authority and then to ensure they are dealt with appropriately.

Although all authorities have to confront strategic management agendas in this sense, not all authorities respond to such agendas strategically! The term 'strategic' implies, inter alia, a carefully-considered position based on proper analysis of the relevant information. Thus it is possible to distinguish between strategic and non-strategic responses to a strategic management agenda! Again epithets like 'intuitive', 'traditional' and 'ad hoc' provide alternative models of response. Or alternatively, strategic choices may be ignored or evaded.

In this book we discuss strategic planning and strategic management, and the interconnection between them, from this strategic choice perspective. In doing so we echo one of the themes of an earlier book in this series which addressed the same topic: *Planning for Change* by Ian Caulfield and John Schultz (1989). We found this book full of helpful insights about the 'state of the art' of strategic planning in the late 1980s, and are happy to acknowledge its influence on our thinking. But things have moved on since, and there is no doubt in our minds that a new book which responds to the changes in strategic agenda and local authority responses since the late 1980s is needed.

Although the book is addressed primarily to practitioners, we hold the view that good practice cannot be divorced from good theory. We have, therefore, included a good deal of material on the historical development of strategic planning, and on its political and organisational context. Anyone in a local authority charged with the development of a strategic initiative can only hope to operate effectively if he or she has a good understanding of the organisational and political dynamics within which such initiatives have to impinge and survive. We make no apologies for blending theory and practice in this way. Strategic planning and management are not topics which can be dealt with in 'handbook' fashion although we are confident that this book also provides a good deal of helpful guidance.

In writing this book, we have drawn on three principal sources. Firstly, we have studied carefully the literature on strategic planning and management, particularly in the local government context, where, in addition to the Caulfield and Schultz volume, we have found the writings of John Stewart on strategy to be particularly helpful. Secondly, to provide a documentary base for the book, we wrote in August 1996 to over 200 authorities in Britain, asking for current examples of strategic planning documents. The authorities approached were all shire counties, metropolitan districts and London boroughs in England; all new unitary authorities in England, Scotland and Wales; together with one in three English shire districts. Over 100 of these authorities responded, almost all of them including relevant documentations (responses were above the 50 per cent average for metropolitan districts, London boroughs and shire districts). That response in itself demonstrates the growing prevalence of strategic approaches. We did not send a follow-up letter, which might have increased the response rate, because we are not concerned in this book to develop a rigorous statistical analysis of current practice, but rather to collect enough evidence to enable us to identify broad trends and to provide material for illustration. One hundred positive responses seemed to us to provide a more than adequate basis for these purposes. Thirdly, we have drawn heavily on our experience – in one case as consultant, in the other as practitioner – working with or in local authorities over the past ten years or so, helping to develop or modify strategic approaches to their corporate operations. The documentation from the survey has enabled us to make sense of what local authorities are *intending* to do. It is only by working with or in a local authority that one can appreciate the 'real world' of strategic planning and management – a world in which strategies face opponents as well as champions – and thereby devise appropriate ways of enhancing their potential effectiveness.

This interplay between theory and practice, and between literature review, current documentation and personal experience is reflected in the book's structure. Because we are aware that 'strategy' as a term is in danger of becoming an over-used buzz-word we felt it would be helpful in Chapter 1 to explore the essence of the term's real meaning, drawing on parallels in everyday life, as well as local government itself. Chapter 2 takes a more normative stance and argues why, in the authors' view, it is particularly important for local authorities to develop explicit strategic choice processes at this point in their history. The urgency of the strategic choice agenda currently facing local authorities is difficult to overstate. In Chapter 3 we identify (and illustrate) a number of key conceptual distinctions, which help to make sense of a range of different activities and outputs in local authorities which are commonly described as 'strategic'. In particular the difference between 'mission statements' (the *way* in which a local authority wishes to operate) and 'strategic visions' (*what* a local authority wishes to do to improve the quality of life within its area) is emphasised. The differences and linkages between levels of strategic choice – role and purpose, corporate issues and service-specific – are also clarified. There follows in Chapter 4 an exploration of the recent historical development and use of strategies, in private and public sector organisations so that it becomes clearer where the current enthusiasm for the idea of strategy in British local government came from. We then in Chapters 5 and 6 explore the real world in which strategic initiatives have to operate. Firstly, the organisational context is examined – what is the potential impact of different types of corporate strategy on other organisational elements like service departments, DSOs and central resource units such as finance and how does this impact affect responses from these quarters to strategic initiatives? Secondly, the political context is explored – in what way do elected members view strategies and how do the latter help or hinder the pursuit of political agendas?

The focus then moves to recent practical experience within British local authorities. Drawing heavily on illustrations from our survey and our own experience, we examine firstly in Chapter 7 the benefits and pitfalls of different approaches to mission statements, and secondly, in Chapter 8 examine strategic visions from the same perspective. In the penultimate chapter the crucial relationship between strategies and budgets is examined, reflecting our belief that one of the key tests of the effectiveness of a corporate strategy is the extent to which it influences budgetary discussions and allocations. Finally, we look at the challenge of implementing strategic initiatives including organisational development, again drawing heavily on personal experience and relevant research to propose a series of 'good practice' guidelines.

Finally, it is important to clarify the personal value perspective from which this book is written. As will already be clear we strongly believe that the development of corporate strategic initiatives is a crucial asset for local authorities, both in helping them to respond to increasingly demanding external and internal agendas, and strengthen their role at a time when traditional justification for elected local government has come under increasing challenge. In that sense we are idealists. But we also try to be realists acknowledging that much that passes for strategic planning is symbolic, ineffective or at worst counterproductive and that what can be achieved in any one authority will depend crucially on its history and traditions, culture, and current political and managerial climate. What might be an appropriate approach in one authority may be quite inappropriate in another. The potential scope of what can be achieved will, in the short term at least, be much greater in some authorities rather than others. Ultimately the most appropriate way in which strategic choices should be identified, consolidated and managed will be unique to each authority. Fortunately there is enough common ground to make a book like this, which necessarily takes an overview, a viable enterprise of potential help to all authorities.

1

The essence of strategy

INTRODUCTION

This is a book about strategic planning and management in local government. These are terms which have come to be used more and more by local authorities over the past ten years or so. Authorities also refer increasingly to strategic visions, strategic issues, strategic monitoring and strategic review as well as to a series of related concepts such as mission statements, core values and policy planning systems. Thus the first key task of a book such as this is to make it clear what is meant by the term strategy and its various applications. We need to identify what is the *essence* of strategy.

One useful starting point in this process of conceptual clarification is to examine how the term strategy is used outside the world of local government, where it is possible to identify a number of different types of usage. It is possible, for example, to apply the term to individuals and to speak of *personal* strategies, although 'life plans' or 'personal development plans' would in this case be more commonly used epithets. There is a familiar use of the term in the field of *sports and games*; football managers, chess players and bridge experts are commonly referred to as having strategies. There is a *military* analogy, in which generals develop and apply strategies to win battles and wars. And there is an increasing widespread use of the term in the *business sector*. Companies devote increasing amounts of time to strategy, as the exponential growth of textbooks on strategic planning and management in the private sector illustrates. By examining all these different uses of the terms, it is possible to build up a picture of the essence of strategy, which can then be applied to the operations of local authorities.

Strategy and individuals

When we refer to strategic choices made by individuals – as identified in personal development plans for example – what kind of choices are involved?

Typically we are talking about the 'big choices' which affect the future course of the individual's career and personal life, opening up some options but closing off others. For example:

- choices about which university to attend and what course of study to undertake;

- choices of partner – typically but not necessarily a marital partner;

- choices of job, both post-qualification and mid-career;

- house purchases and sales;

- acquisition of new professional skills or further qualifications;

- choice of when to start a family and, subsequently, to add to it;

- moves from one part of the country to another.

What do these big issues – or, in our terminology, strategic choices – have in common?

- They typically involve or imply a significant *commitment of resources* (often, but not necessarily, financial resources). The impact of a house purchase through a mortgage, or the costs of retraining mid-career provide vivid illustrations.

- Once taken, they can only be *reversed with difficulty* and at significant financial/personal cost. The problems of reversibility of strategic personal choices can be illustrated by a marriage which ends in divorce, with its associated financial (and personal) costs, and the time it usually takes to complete the process.

- They are often *difficult choices* in which advantages and disadvantages have to be carefully weighed up. Although some people would argue that their choices of partner or job were in no sense difficult ones to make – there was no doubt (beyond a certain point) what they wanted to do, or whom they wanted to marry – it is perhaps more common for a 'big choice' to be one which does engender a certain amount of agonising.

- They open up a *range of opportunities* but foreclose others. If someone joins a school of architecture at a university and subsequently qualifies as an architect, that outcome makes possible a whole range of different types of jobs which require architectural skills, but defines out those jobs associated with other professional qualifications and skills (e.g. accountancy).

- They provide a framework for a *host of detailed decisions* and activities which flow from each big choice. The purchase of a particular house in a particular area generates a range of detailed decisions and actions in relation to matters such as mortgage repayments, house insurance, house and garden maintenance and choice of school.

- They are fundamental in contributing to or hindering the *overall well-being* of the individual. One only has to think of the difference between a happy and unhappy marriage, or a satisfying and unsatisfying job to one's quality of life.

Consider the dilemma of someone who sees advantage in a move to a better-paid higher status job in another part of the country, but is concerned about the impact of 'uprooting' his or her family. Or someone who desperately wants to change direction in career terms, but cannot see how he or she can manage financially during the transition period. This final example illustrates a further important characteristic of personal strategic choices – they are often interconnected. Decisions about job moves are made in the light of possible impact on a marriage/family. Decisions about house purchases may affect decisions about whether or not to start a family.

We are not suggesting that 'big choices' such as those illustrated are always identified as such, or made in a rational way (i.e. with a careful attempt to assess future costs, benefits and impacts on other big choices). People can drift into and out of relationships, change jobs impulsively, buy houses with mortgage repayment implications that they cannot subsequently sustain, or start families in an accidental rather than a planned way. What the personal development plans assume is that future well-being is *more* likely to be enhanced by the rational analysis and planning of such choices than by drift, impulse or accident.

As we will demonstrate during the course of this book, all these characteristics of personal strategies are applicable in principle to strategic approaches in local authorities. The way in which we have characterised strategic choices of individuals – where the right choice is often difficult to identify but which, once made, has major consequences for future well-being, involves significant commitment of resources and can only be reversed with difficulty – matches the typical content of the strategic agenda of local authorities. For authorities, as well as individuals, strategic choices open up some possibilities, foreclose others, and influence a whole series of subsequent more detailed decisions. The strategic agendas of local authorities as with those of individuals, imply the necessity to assess and allow for the influence of one strategic choice on another. While some local authorities make explicit the strategic choice process and address it as rationally and systematically as possible (as do some individuals) others do not, *reacting* instead to external challenges and pressures on an ad-hoc or 'gut reaction' basis. It is arguable that the latter types of

> **The strategic agendas of authorities imply the necessity to assess the influence of one strategic choice on another.**

response are as sub-optimal for the long-term welfare of local authorities as they are for individuals (although the existence of a literature which argues that this is not the case (*see* Lindblom 1959; Wildavsky 1975) has to be recognised).

Strategy and games

As every follower of association football will know football managers have – or purport to have – strategies. Their strategies typically involve some kind of team formation 4–2–4, 4–4–2, the use (or non-use) of sweepers, overlapping full-backs, one or more wingers etc. In addition, strategies for individual games take on board an assessment of the strengths and weaknesses of the opposition, and typically modify or apply the normal way of playing to respond to such strengths and weaknesses e.g. close-marking of creative midfielders, exposure of identified defensive weaknesses.

In the game itself, strategies are expressed through the use of more specific tactics e.g. 'set-pieces' for corners, or free-kick routines within striking distance of the opponent's goal, or the use of offside-traps. As the game progresses, tactics – or indeed the strategy itself – may be changed in response to outcomes. A manager whose side is 2–0 down at half-time may well consider changing the formation of his side (a strategic change) as well as changing its tactics (more long balls to the tall strikers). There is a possibility that he will have anticipated such a situation and prepared a contingency plan in advance to respond to it. Similar parallels in relation to game plans, contingency plans, strategy and tactics can be identified in other team sports, in 'partner' card games such as contract bridge, and in individual contests such as chess and lawn tennis. A similar set of concepts is also utilised in warfare, where the sense of the strategy/tactics relationship is perhaps most highly developed.

The notion of strategy in the context of games, although it has similarities with personal strategies, also has differences. What it adds to our understanding of the term is an awareness of the dynamic and often unpredictable *context* in which strategy is applied. In this context, contingency plans have to be prepared, and strategy/tactics modified if outcomes prove unsatisfactory. In addition, there is a stronger emphasis on the link between the key choices (strategy) and the way such choices are implemented (detail), with the two processes operating in reciprocal inter-relationship.

Local authorities too face a dynamic, unpredictable and sometimes hostile environment, which emphasises the need for adaptability and change. The need for strategic review, changes of tactics or contingency planning to cope with actual or anticipated changes in external circumstances (or in central government strategies) is well demonstrated by the recent history of local government. Battles over the attempts by central government to control the expenditure of individual local authorities in the mid-1980s; responding to the by no means explicit changes in the 'rules of the game' of the recent Local Government Review; and reviewing a strategy of maximum in-house retention of services in the light of the unexpected loss of contracts to external agencies under compulsory competitive tendering (CCT) all provide illustrations of the relevance of the 'games' analogies. When we come to consider recent changes in the way local authorities have approached 'strategy', it will be apparent that the implications of the current context of local government have increasingly been recognised. There is less reliance on 'tablets of stone' and a correspondingly greater readiness to adopt or change strategy without shedding the *key* values and principles underlying it.

Strategy and private sector organisations

Strategic planning and management have long been deployed by private sector organisations. At a recent local authority seminar organised by one of the authors, a guest speaker – the managing director of a successful locally based company specialising in personnel recruitment and staff training services – expressed amazement at the fact that the authority concerned was only now (in 1994) recognising the importance of strategic planning, and wondered how it had operated before? His view was that private firms which did not put time and energy into strategic planning would fall by the wayside. He and his senior management team spent three to four days every year closeted in a comfortable hotel, sorting out the strategic plan for the coming year.

What do private companies mean by strategy? In this context, the term involves the analysis of trends in the sales of various products and services, an assessment of market opportunities and likely competition, and the development of a product/market portfolio for the next year, which may

5

involve a combination of existing, modified or new products or services. It may involve withdrawing other products or services depending on an assessment of market demand and market opportunities, or it may imply attempts to acquire other companies and/or to sell off particular subsidiaries. As with personal strategic activity it is an attempt to look ahead, identify the big issues and choices, and to decide what to do about them.

Do local authorities have anything to learn from this kind of strategic activity? Fifteen years ago the business analogy would probably have been seen as of limited applicability. Today, given the advent of CCT and the increasing severity of the financial crises facing local authorities under the present system of universal council tax capping, the business analogy is of much greater relevance. Local authorities are increasingly having to ask difficult questions about whether they can afford to provide services which are not mandatory, or at the very least to which services of this nature they wish to give the highest priority and protect. Parallel 'private sector' choices exist about whether to retain blue-collar and now white-collar services which are subject to CCT 'in house', or whether the authority is happy to see them provided by external agencies (or, alternatively, which services are viewed as particularly important subjects for in-house retention).

To us, the surprise of the managing director in the example referred to above was well-justified. If private companies involved in producing, marketing and selling perhaps five or six different lines or products think strategy is important, then how much more important it is for a local authority which not only has to provide, in all probability a much wider range of products/services, but cannot operate through the logic of the market in a way a private business can. Much of a local authority's work is involved in assessing and meeting need which is neither expressed nor met through the 'market'. If one recognises in addition the increasingly wide-ranging agenda of issues which are being tackled by local authorities who are attempting to play a 'community governance' role, then the crucial importance of strategic planning and management in a local government context is further highlighted.

Developing a view of the 'essence of strategy'

By reviewing the meaning and significance of strategy in personal life, competitive games and private companies, it has been possible to build up a composite picture of the key characteristics of 'strategy' based largely on everyday uses of the term. It is helpful to summarise these key characteristics. Strategic choices are typically the *difficult choices* concerning the *big issues* (facing individuals, football managers, or private companies) with implications for future welfare or success. As such they are to be distinguished from the much larger number of more detailed day-to-day decisions made by individuals many of which are contingent upon or follow from strategic choices. More detailed decisions made explicitly in pursuance of a strategic goal are often termed *tactical* choices. Strategic choices involve looking into the future and assessing longer-term implications of current trends and longer-term consequence of possible options. One big choice will often impinge upon others; it will often, therefore, be important to explore the *inter-relationships* between them. Strategic choices usually involve a major commitment of services and are reversible only with difficulty. Some individuals, football managers, or companies expend a good deal of energy identifying and analysing strategic choices. Others do not do so, and respond to the big issues facing them in other ways either in a traditional, impulsive or evasive way.

This composite picture is equally applicable in principle to the role of strategy in the operations of local authorities. The distinction between strategic and operational management has been helpfully encapsulated by John Stewart (1995a, p. 67) in a table that reflects several of the distinctions which we have already made.

Strategic management	Operational management
■ Long-term perspective.	■ Short-term perspective.
■ Exposes choices.	■ Reinforces continuities.
■ Guided by political values.	■ Expresses professional concerns.
■ Developed in an organisational pause.	■ Continuous activity.
■ Grounded in the environment.	■ Grounded in the organisation.
■ Looks outward to impact.	■ Concerned with activity.
■ Looks to a network of community organisations.	■ Limited by organisational boundaries.
■ Sees inter-relationships between tasks.	■ Task-centred.
■ Aware of uncertainty.	■ Certain of continuity.

Local authorities, too, may choose to identify and explicitly address strategic agendas, or may choose to marginalise or ignore them. Our argument is that strategic choices face all local authorities; but whether they are recognised as such, and responded to strategically is an open question. One of the main aims of this book is to persuade local authorities that there are considerable potential benefits in recognising, and expending time and energy in addressing the strategic agendas facing them.

> **Strategic choices face all local authorities but whether they are responded to strategically is an open question.**

SUMMARY

By considering the use of the term strategy in relation to personal life, games, warfare and the private sector, it is possible to develop a 'common sense' list of the essential characteristics of strategy, which are in principle applicable to the role of strategy in the operations of local authorities. These essential characteristics of strategy, may be summarised as follows.

- Strategic issues are the 'big choices' which are fundamental to the future well-being of the individual or organisation.

- They usually involve a considerable commitment of resources.

- They are only reversible with difficulty and through an equivalent expenditure of resources.

- They involve difficult choices where there are one or more plausible alternatives, the advantages and disadvantages of which have to be carefully weighed up.

- They open up a range of possibilities, but foreclose a number of others.

- They provide a framework and a direction for a host of detailed decisions.

- Strategies are applied in a context which is dynamic and often unpredictable, and will often require modification. In this context the value of 'contingency plans' is apparent.

- Strategy is about choosing not to continue with existing activities, as well as initiating new ones.

- Although all individuals and organisations face a changing agenda of strategic choices, such choices are not necessarily responded to in a strategic manner! It is possible to make a non-strategic response to a strategic choice!

2

The current case for corporate strategy in local government

INTRODUCTION

As it was set out in Chapter 1, the argument in principle for a strategic approach in local government sounds very much like common sense. Facing up to the big issues, tackling the difficult choices, setting a direction for the authority as a whole, all these activities sound like eminently sensible ideas for local authorities to undertake.

In fact the case for corporate strategy in local authorities is not quite as self-evident as this! There is a salutary lesson to be learned in this respect from the relative failure of corporate planning/management in the years following the 1974 local government reorganisation. Despite powerful pressure from official advisory committees (the Bains Committee) and academics (notably John Stewart and his colleagues at the increasingly influential Institute of Local Government Studies) corporate strategies rarely moved beyond the status of impressive (or sometimes not so impressive) documents to processes which were central to an authority's operations.

Caulfield and Schultz (1989) examine some of the reasons for the relative failure of the so-called 'corporate planning movement': the process was rarely initiated by politicians, nor did it relate to political priorities or agendas; many of the corporate plans were too ambitious, with ill-advised aspirations towards comprehensiveness; there was a lack of prioritisation amongst objectives, and far too much detail. But none of these shortcomings are inevitable. It is our argument that they have been avoided by increasing numbers of authorities in the mid-1990s.

A comparison between the case for strategy in the 1970s and the 1990s

There was a further important reason why corporate strategies did not 'take off' in the late 1970s – the climate in which local government operated then was very different from that of today. Firstly, although 1976 marked the year of 'the end of the party' (to use Anthony Crosland's immortal phrase) as far as local government was concerned, the financial pressures on local authorities were of a different order of magnitude to those which developed in the 1980s and 1990s. Secondly, the dominant ethos of local authorities was still that of 'service provision', with the corporate agenda typically focusing on the inter-relationship between statutory services, rather than the more wide-ranging interventionist corporate agendas addressed by many local authorities today. The economic development role in local government was then at an embryonic stage, environmental conservation and greening issues were scarcely on the agenda and community safety was a concern which was typically seen as an issue for the police authority.

Client/contractor distinctions were not yet being seriously addressed. If a local authority had responsibility for a service, it usually chose to provide that service itself. Powerful service departments and committees dominated local authorities much more than they do today. A corporate strategic agenda had to find a niche in this service-dominated world and frequently failed to do so.

Thus in a traditional county council in the late 1970s, for example, with little ambition to move beyond the provision of statutory services, whose structure was dominated by service departments and committees, and whose annual budget process was dominated by inter-committee battles over the distribution of the annual budgetary increment, the case for a corporate strategy was by no means self-evident. What added value could it have contributed in the kind of circumstances set out above? The realistic answer was 'not a great deal'!

The climate in which local authorities operate has however been transformed in the intervening period, with a concomitant change in the choices faced. Gone are the old certainties concerning the public benefits of good professional practice, the annual budgetary increment, the self-sufficiency paradigm in relation to service provision, and the blurring of client and contractor rules. In the mid-1990s, the climate facing all local authorities includes the following elements:

- severe central government-imposed financial constraint, reaching crisis proportions in increasing numbers of authorities and in the vast majority implying the need for real cuts in expenditure;

- the requirement to introduce client/contractor or purchaser/provider distinctions in an increasing range of service areas, resulting in an increasing challenge to the self-sufficiency of traditional service departments and sometimes leading to a business-unit dominated form of organisational structure;

- an expectation that local authorities should operate more entrepreneurially in partnership (or through contracts) with a wider range of external organisations whether public, private or voluntary sector to respond to local issues;

- a wider scope and greater degree of explicitness within the local manifestos and policy agendas of *all* the major parties (although there has admittedly been some retreat in this respect from the 'socialism in one borough' rhetoric of the mid-1980s).

It is our argument that the collective impact of all these forces has been to fundamentally change the case for the introduction of a corporate strategy dimension into the affairs of local authorities, from an 'optional extra' to a necessity. The interplay of the four processes identified above: financial constraint/crisis; the fragmentation of service roles; the enhanced entrepreneurial dimension involving closer links with external organisations; and the growing explicitness (and breadth) of political agendas has resulted in the opening up of a number of fundamental choices regarding the very role and purpose of local authorities. The process has been highlighted in a recent LGMB publication *Fitness for Purpose*.

> **The collective impact of all these forces has been to fundamentally change the case for the introduction of a corporate strategy from an 'optional extra' to a necessity.**

Strategic choices about role and purpose

In *Fitness for Purpose* it is argued that there are three key dimensions to the choices facing local authorities:

- the extent to which the local authority wishes to exercise a wider role in local governance;

- the degree to which the authority wants to introduce market mechanisms into its operations;

- the relative importance the local authority puts on service to individuals and service to communities, and the meaning it gives to 'community'.

Local governance

A local authority that emphasises local governance will concern itself with a wide range of problems and issues in its area. Such an authority might identify a comprehensive range of local needs, prioritise them, and use whatever means are appropriate to meet these needs. These could include direct or contracted-out service provision, inspection and regulation, and channels of influence and advocacy.

An authority that places less emphasis on local governance might choose to concentrate primarily on its responsibilities for ensuring the delivery of services. It would therefore extend its activities to matters of wider concern only when under public pressure to do so.

Neither approach is right or wrong, it is a matter of interpretation. Both approaches are feasible in current circumstances, but the former involves a more comprehensive, proactive and interventionist interpretation of local governance than the latter.

Market mechanisms

The second strategic choice concerns the role of market mechanisms, including competition and contracting out, in the operations of the local authority. While these have become increasingly important as a result of governmental legislation, local authorities can still exercise choice in how they incorporate market mechanisms into their operations beyond the requirements of statute.

At one end of the spectrum are authorities that have attempted to maximise the role of market mechanisms. In some cases, they have gone well beyond what they are required to do, believing this to be the best path to efficient and effective service provision.

At the other end of the spectrum there are authorities which believe that the best way of providing efficient services in a wide range of circumstances is through direct public provision by the authority itself. While following the letter of the law, they exercise their powers of choice to minimise the role of market mechanisms in their operations and to retain as far as possible direct service provision.

Again it is not being suggested that one choice is better or worse than the other. The point is simply that different choices are possible and that many authorities have made their choice.

Individuals or communities

The third strategic choice is the authority's perception of the nature of the population it serves. There are authorities that emphasise the needs and preferences of individuals and/or household units, seeing their role as serving consumers, customers or service clients.

Other authorities, while not denying the significance of individual and household needs, emphasise their role in meeting the needs of wider communities. They may be based on localities such as a city, county, town or neighbourhood. Or they may be based on groups sharing common interests such as class, ethnicity or a common cause. Where an emphasis is placed on the community, the local authority faces a further choice over the relative importance attached to communities of interest and of place, and within the latter upon the authority-wide community or the neighbourhood.

As with the other two dimensions there is no right choice; indeed an authority may seek a balance between these emphases. What is clear to us is that these choices are real ones, which local authorities face, and which lead to very different structures, processes and culture, depending upon the combination of choice made.

The wider strategic agenda

Strategic choices at this level are in fact but one part of the strategic agenda facing local authorities. There are other incentives which stem from the current turbulent climate (see above) facing local authorities.

- Even for an authority which has little interest in playing a wider governance role, there are hard choices to be made as to which services are to be protected and which reduced or even discontinued. Incrementalist or 'bargaining power' approaches, which may be an acceptable way of dealing with expenditure *increments*, are less likely to be acceptable in relation to expenditure. Prioritisation becomes essential; the issue is *how* priorities are decided.

- Entrepreneurship, opportunity-taking, and negotiation with external bodies are all activities which imply a clear sense of a 'desired future direction'. Without this sense of direction, and its associated corporate objectives, it is difficult to assess which opportunities should be taken and which refused, or what outcome is sought from negotiations with an external organisation. An out-of-town shopping centre proposal may be an opportunity to be grasped or avoided, depending upon its potential contribution to the council's strategic objectives. And in any negotiation situation the party with the clearest ideas of what its preferred (and acceptable) outcomes are, coupled with appropriate negotiation skills, is in a strong position.

■ Outward-looking 'governmental' political agendas – as set out in party manifestos – are rarely implementable as they stand. Typically they require clarification, prioritisation and co-ordination if they are to impinge coherently upon the decision-making processes of the council. Although a strategic objective does not necessarily imply the allocation of financial resources, in reality there are often expenditure implications. This means that strategic objectives are often competing with one another for (increasingly scarce) 'new development' resources, not to mention the competition with existing services.

■ In addition, strategic priorities invariably have implications for one another. The pursuit of environmental enhancement objectives may hinder the achievement of economic development/job creation initiatives and vice versa. Without a corporate strategy it is difficult to see how such prioritisation requirements, opportunity costs and inter-connected impacts can be taken account of.

There is a further important argument for corporate strategy. At a time when the status of local government as an institution has been threatened by central government disparagement and disempowerment, and local indifference (as epitomised, for example, by the obstinately resilient level of less than 40 per cent voter turnout at local elections) any initiative which has the potential to strengthen the relationship between a local authority and its electorate, and hence enhance the credibility and status of local government, is to be welcomed. Some authorities who have gone down the corporate strategy route have chosen to consult the public in the process and have reported an encouraging level of public interest and involvement (*see* Chapter 10 for further details).

In summary, the case for corporate strategy is captured by the old adage 'if you don't know where you're going, you're unlikely to arrive there!' For a local authority content to be little more than the sum of its departmental parts, the case for service strategies is likely to be seen as stronger than the case for a corporate strategy. However, the competing expenditure claims of service strategies – which invariably contain an element of the 'bid document' about them – will have to be resolved by some means or other in such authorities. There are increasingly difficult service prioritisation choices facing this type of local authority. For authorities which have adopted a community governance perspective, although the case for service strategies does not diminish, the argument for corporate strategy becomes overwhelming.

Much has been written recently about the impact of fragmentation on local government. Fragmentation has both an internal and external dimension. The internal dimension reflects the way in which local authorities are being required to 'separate out' internal functions – e.g. client/contractor – and reflect these distinctions structurally in a way for which there was little precedent before 1980. The external dimension reflects the way in which some responsibilities which used to rest with local authorities have over the past ten years been transferred to other agencies (e.g. higher and further education, grant-maintained schools, training schemes) with which, however, authorities are required to co-ordinate or

> **Strategy is arguably the most important potential antidote to fragmentation.**

jointly plan their remaining responsibilities. Both these processes have increased the process of *differentiation* within local authorities themselves, and within the field of local governance in which local authorities play a less dominant role than was previously the case, but in which they remain the only authorities with the legitimacy and accountability to provide a local 'overview'. In these circumstances, the case for integrative devices (to counter the fragmentary input of differentiation) becomes increasingly powerful. Strategy – in its various forms – is one such device, indeed arguably the most important potential antidote to fragmentation.

The spread of corporate strategies

So far, our approach has been to argue the case for corporate strategy on *a priori* grounds, referring to the circumstances in which local authorities operate and the nature of the choices facing them. These circumstances and choices are such that local authorities can only become shapers of their destiny if they introduce a dimension of corporate strategic thinking into their operations. Otherwise they run the risk of becoming de facto 'firefighting' authorities, dealing with a series of external pressures on a disjointed or ad hoc basis.

What evidence is there that local authorities have themselves recognised and responded to these arguments? The LGMB Survey of Internal Organisational

Change in Local Government (Young and Mills 1993) shows that there has been a growing strategic awareness. Of the 285 councils surveyed, although 24 per cent had neither considered nor adopted a corporate or strategic plan, 28 per cent were considering preparing or adopting one and 48 per cent had done so. The survey also documented a steady increase in the adoption of strategic plans during the late 1980s and early 1990s. Similar patterns were recorded for the adoption of mission or 'core values' statements (59 per cent of all authorities surveyed had adopted such documents by 1992). The recent update of the 1993 survey shows a significant increase in this activity between 1992 and 1995 (Young and Mills 1997).

Clearly increasing numbers of authorities have recognised the argument of Clarke and Stewart (1988, p.14), about the heightened case for strategy in enabling authorities.

> *The enabling Council needs a strategy to guide its approach. The need is, if anything, greater than for an authority which acts directly. An enabling authority works with and through other organisations: without a strategy, the authority's aims and objectives can easily be taken over by those with which it works.*

SUMMARY

For a multi-purpose governmental agency there is at any time an argument for developing a corporate strategy. The argument is, however, particularly strong for British local authorities in the late 1990s for the following reasons:

- severe central government-imposed financial constraints, implying in most authorities the need for real cuts in expenditure;

- an increasing move towards 'community governance' i.e. the concern of local authorities to respond to a wide range of local issues;

- an increasing enthusiasm on the part of authorities for entrepreneurial activity, in partnership with a wide range of other local bodies;

- the opening-up of a range of choices regarding the role and purpose of local authorities, in the wake of the government's post 1987 legislation programme;

- the adverse impact of fragmentation on the cohesiveness of local authorities;

- the need to re-establish the perceived value of local government in local communities.

3

The dimensions of corporate strategy

INTRODUCTION

In the previous chapters we have tried to clarify what it means in principle to introduce a 'strategic' dimension into the corporate working of a local authority, and explain why it has become increasingly important over the past ten years or so that local authorities should do so. But so far, the arguments have been at a relatively general level. It is time to explore in more detail what the adoption of a strategic approach actually involves. What should a local authority which recognises the importance of moving in this direction actually do about it? In this chapter we set out and discuss the main dimensions of corporate strategy.

The scope of strategic choices

It was emphasised in the introduction that the strategy is about *choice*, in relation to the big issues facing a local authority as a corporate entity. What kind of choices are we talking about here? Six different types of choice are set out below which can legitimately be described as 'strategic', in that they affect the future well-being and effectiveness of the authority and have significant resource implications.

1. Choices to *prioritise organisational resources in meeting objectives* of perceived significance. Such choices are capable of organisation and expression in a documentary form (or strategic plan), and reflect '*What* we want to achieve'.

2. Choices *between alternative means for achieving such objectives*. These choices are also capable of organisation and expression in a documentary form (or strategic plan) and involve substantive policy objectives.

3. Choices of *priority between such objectives* when a conflict or mismatch becomes apparent. These choices too can be expressed in a documentary form (or strategic plan).

4. Choices of which *cultural attributes* the authority wishes to adopt and express. These choices are capable of organisation and expression in a documentary form, and reflect '*how* we want to operate'.

5. Choices made in *response to an unanticipated crisis* or externally generated pressure for action.

6. Choices of *organisational action* – how an authority is *managed* to facilitate the above five choices.

It is important therefore to distinguish between:

- strategic *planning* and strategic *management*;
- *proactive* strategic choice and *reactive* strategic choice;
- *substantive* strategic issues (what) and *cultural* strategic issues (how);
- different organisational levels of strategic application: role and purpose, authority-wide priorities, and service priorities.

These key distinctions are explored in more detail below.

Strategic planning and strategic management

Strategic planning is a process whereby a local authority consciously sets out to identify priorities for its future activities, through a process of clarification of its objectives or the key problems facing it and an analysis of both the opportunities for achieving those objectives and the barriers to be overcome. Such a process usually results in the drawing up and publication of a strategic (corporate) plan.

Strategic management, on the other hand has three different but related meanings. Firstly, in a proactive sense, the term can be used to refer to the way in which the corporate strategy is managed, for example the way in which the strategy is reviewed, updated and monitored, and the way in which action is taken to achieve strategic objectives or reduce strategic problems. Because of the political significance of a corporate strategy, strategic management

> Because of the political significance of a corporate strategy, strategic management is inherently a political management process.

in this sense is inherently a political management process. Secondly, it can refer to the process of changing the organisational culture or structure to facilitate or reflect strategic priorities. In this case, the process is more dominated by managerial considerations (although politicians will have a legitimate interest). Thirdly, it can reflect the distinction between reactive and proactive strategic choice.

Proactive and reactive strategic choice

The first view of strategic management implies the prior existence of a corporate strategy or at least a strategic planning process. Many authorities have not chosen to produce such a document or to develop such a process. Some corporate strategies although 'in existence' have ceased to be influential as a guide to corporate action. Yet such authorities will still face a series of big choices: whether to argue for unitary status or a continuation of the two-tier system in the recent Local Government Review; how to respond to pressures for opting out amongst a number of local schools; what to do about a locally controversial health authority's proposals to close a local hospital. In this alternative, reactive sense strategic management refers to the way in which such big choices are responded to, involving some form of assessment of the potential advantages and disadvantages to the local authority of different options with at least a medium-term time perspective. The point to emphasise in relation to this distinction is that the vast majority of local authorities practise strategic management in a reactive sense, even if they do not involve themselves in the proactive process of strategic planning.

Local authorities which operate proactive strategy planning processes will of course also have to react to big choices not identified in their most recent review of issues and priorities. The turbulence and unpredictability of the operating environment of local authorities over the past 20 years has made this reactive element in strategic management inevitable. One of the key arguments of this book, however, is that the operation of a proactive strategic planning process, to which there is real political and senior management commitment, provides a framework which informs and facilitates 'reactive' strategic

> **The turbulence and unpredictability of the operating environment has made this reactive element in strategic management inevitable.**

management. Responses to unforeseen strategic choices can be made in a non-strategic fashion, or they can be made strategically, with a proper assessment of long-term consequences. The 'added value' of making such choices within the context of an existing corporate strategy is that the issue can be methodically considered in relation to a wider agenda of strategic priorities in the authority.

Levels of strategic choice

Strategic choices can be identified at three different levels of local authority activity.

1. Strategic choices about the authority's role and purpose.

2. Strategic choices about an authority's priorities for action.

3. Strategic choices about a particular service carried out by the authority.

These levels of choice are inter-related and although listed in logical sequence, there is no suggestion that they should necessarily be addressed sequentially.

Role and purpose

Strategic choices about a local authority's role and purpose were discussed and illustrated in Chapter 2. We argued that choices could be identified along three major dimensions:

1. governance/service provision;

2. markets/public provision;

3. individual-orientation/community-orientation.

It is possible to take this choice process further and identify (as was done in *Fitness for Purpose*) four different types of local authority which resulted from different contributions of choice in relation to the above three dimensions. These types can be identified as *direct service provision*, *commercialism*, *community governance* and the *neighbourhood approach*. They are characterised in Fig. 3.1.

It is even possible to identify each of the four 'ideal types': the London Borough of Brent under Conservative control has been a recent enthusiast for the commercialist approach; the London Borough of Tower Hamlets, under Liberal Democrat control, developed the neighbourhood approach in a radical way; and the City of Birmingham has long pursued policies designed to establish it as a city of 'international status'. While the more traditional direct service provision emphasis is by definition less newsworthy, we do not think

1. The authority with an emphasis on direct service provision.
   'There is great strength in the traditional approach to local governance and service delivery. This approach can and should be revised to pay greater attention to the needs of customers. There is scope for the introduction of market mechanisms, but the scope should not be over-emphasised. The introduction of such mechanisms should not be used as a reason for the radical redesign of organisational structures, processes and personnel policies, which should remain rooted in an ethos of direct public provision.'

2. The authority with an emphasis on a commercial approach.
   'Although there are some issues which require council action on behalf of the residents of the area as a whole, the main raison d'etre of local government is to ensure the provision of an appropriate range of local services which cannot be provided directly by the market. Such service can in general be provided most cost-effectively by maximising the role of the private sector in the provision of service, and by stimulating a commercial approach within the authority itself.'

3. The authority with an emphasis on community governance.
   'The main task of a local authority is to identify the needs of the area it represents and to do all it can to meet those needs. It should be prepared to use direct provision, and to work with a wide range of external organisations – public, private and voluntary – to meet those needs, depending on what is most effective in the circumstances. It should play a pro-active leadership role.'

4. The authority with an emphasis on a neighbourhood approach.
   'Many important local choices cannot be made on the basis of the summation of individual preferences, but require discussion and resolution at a collective level. Although some collective choices are authority-wide, a council should recognise the significance and diversity of the different local communities within its area. Its structures, processes and personnel policies should reflect this emphasis on communities.'

Fig. 3.1 Four cameos of local authority role and purpose

most readers will have much difficulty identifying examples from their own localities!

The main point is that it is currently possible to identify an agenda of strategic choices in relation to a local authority's role and purpose. The agenda is always open to change through the action of central government and reaction of local authorities. Our argument is that an important part of the strategy planning process for all local authorities is to address key choices of role and purpose and to make it explicit where the authority stands. Such explicitness will undoubtedly clarify and facilitate the choice process in relation to the other two levels identified: services/topic areas and priorities for action.

Service strategies

There is a logic in starting a strategic planning process by addressing 'role and purpose' issues, because so much is implied for the other levels of strategic choice by a clarification of such choices. However there are always dangers in an over-emphasis on 'top-down' approaches and its not always easy, as we shall see, to persuade elected members to address a 'role and purpose' agenda. In a hung or balanced authority (unless there exists a formal or 'de facto' coalition) it becomes increasingly unlikely that a majority of councillors would agree on one. In such authorities it may be more realistic to operate the corporate strategy process 'from the bottom up'. Even in authorities where it is possible to address 'role and purpose' choices politically, there are advantages in a parallel process which addresses strategic choices in relation to service and topic issues.

In relation to the specific service areas in which local authorities have a primary responsibility (e.g. social services, land-use planning, housing, education and recreation) strategic planning is typically a familiar and well-established process. In some cases the process is underpinned by a legislative requirement, often operated in conjunction with a resource allocation system. Housing Investment Plans (HIPs) and Transportation Policies and Plans (TPPs) are perhaps the two best-known examples but there are several other manifestations such as Community Care Plans (social services/health), Policing Plans, Structure Plans and Unitary Development Plans (which are in effect statute-based land use planning strategies).

Above and beyond such legislative requirements, many authorities have established systems of 'service plans' whereby each major service committee is expected to produce a long or medium term plan outlining its objectives, priorities, mechanisms of implementation and sometimes the financial implications of the plan content. Sometimes these documents are known as 'business plans' although that term is best reserved for the financial details of service financing, charging and performance targets, once objectives and priorities have been decided.

Service strategies can be used in one of two different ways, depending upon whether or not a corporate strategy exists. In the absence of a corporate strategy, it is common for service strategies to be used as *bid* documents, making a reasoned case for expenditure on the service in question. It is then possible in such an authority to develop a corporate strategy by comparing the service bid documents and allocating resources in relation to the relative strength of the cases presented, although this approach would only be appropriate in an authority committed to a service-provision or opposed to a governance role. There are of course various bargaining-based resource allocation methods much less dependent on logical argument which can be used in the budget process.

Alternatively service strategies may be expected to take as a starting point a corporate strategy, in other words, an expectation that the service committee should develop a service strategy in the light of the authority's corporate priorities/objectives. In this case the service strategy would be expected to show how different existing service elements contribute to corporate priorities, or to develop new service initiatives which so contribute.

The characteristics of strategies as outlined in Chapter 1 and the case for their use as developed in Chapter 2 are equally applicable to services except perhaps in cases where service demand is predictable and service provision is non-competitive (e.g. cemeteries/crematoria). Because this is a book about corporate strategy, the key issue for us is the relationship between service strategies and corporate strategy. A *'de minimis'* concept of corporate strategy is one which allocates resources between service areas in response to the cases made in the service strategies. In more governmental conceptions of corporate strategy, however, their scope is far greater than this.

Authority-wide priorities for action

It is the middle level of strategic activity – setting priorities for action – which contributes the dominant focus for corporate strategy. Strategic choice in relation to role and purpose certainly forms part of corporate strategy, but operates at a relatively high level of generality and is perhaps most important in setting a framework for more specific strategic choices at level two. Strategic choices in relation to services may in certain circumstances be drawn within a genuinely corporate strategy (see above) but in most cases fall outside it. Authority-wide priorities for action can at best both reflect and implement choices made in relation to role and purpose and provide a basis for integrating strategic activity in relation to specific services (and to specific topic areas – see below). Three separate elements of strategic priorities for action can be identified:

1. *Core values*, which are expressions of the desired *culture* of the authority, the way it wishes to behave in relation to its own staff, the public, outside organisations. The term 'mission statement' is often used to label the document which expresses the core values.

2. *A strategic vision*, which sets out the *agenda of problems, issues or objectives* which the authority wishes to address, and which transcends the duties and activities in relation to specific services within the organisation.

3. *Strategic responses*, which constitute the unavoidable '*reactive*' element of corporate strategy – how to respond to the *unanticipated* issues which impinge upon the authority on a regular basis (e.g. the announcement of the intention to close an industrial plant which forms a key element in the local economy).

By definition, the kind of issues which develop suddenly cannot be treated in the same way as strategic issues which have already been incorporated into a corporate strategy, although they can of course be included at the time of the next strategic review. Although the existing corporate strategy may provide indications of how the new issues should be responded to, in many cases such guidance will be very limited, and initially at least the issue will have to be treated on a relatively isolated basis. What is important in these circumstances is that the authority has the management capacity to recognise such issues, relate them (where appropriate) to the existing corporate strategy and to develop an appropriate response. In other words strategic responsiveness is often a test of strategic *management* rather than strategic *planning*. One of the key implications, however, of this need for a strategic response capacity is the need to regularly update corporate strategies. A strategic agenda established in May 1996 is unlikely to survive intact until May 1997. New challenges may emerge while previous priorities may decrease in importance. However, some elements of the corporate strategy such as statements of role and purpose and core values – can be expected to have a longer survival time.

Strategic visions are typically comprised of a series of strategic issues based on particular topics, and may indeed have been developed through a process of accretion of topic-specific strategies. By topic-based strategies we mean strategies developed by a local authority in relation to issues which cannot be subsumed within the confines of a particular department, but to which the authority nonetheless wishes to devote attention and resources (labelled as 'wicked issues' by John Stewart (1995a, p. 40)). These are by definition 'corporate' issues in that there is normally little or no statutory responsibility to deal with them, and/or they typically imply action by more than one existing department. Economic regeneration, environmental conservation/

sustainability and 'healthy cities' are three prevalent recent examples. Typically they reflect political priorities, and represent topics in which politicians can see the value of strategic planning, even where they are not convinced of the need for a more wide-ranging strategic initiative. Also, in the case of hung or balanced authorities, it is sometimes possible to identify enough inter-party agreement to develop a strategic initiative on one or more special topics, while agreement on an authority-wide set of strategic priorities would be unrealistic. In both cases, it makes sense to develop topic-based strategies both because it is advantageous in itself, but also because it may subsequently prove possible to draw together a range of such topic-based initiatives into a more wide-ranging set of priorities. Although there is a logic for developing such a set of priorities first, there will be many circumstances where a topic by topic approach is the most appropriate and indeed the only possible way forward.

Different approaches to strategic agendas

In relation to *substantive* strategic agendas – attempts to set out in an inter-related way what the authority wishes to do over the next five to fifty years – three different approaches can be identified in the current practice of local authorities:

1. *Comprehensive approaches*: These involve the establishment of a set of corporate priorities which address all the issues to which the authority wishes to respond at a particular point in time, as an initial and separate stage in the corporate planning process.

   They are comprehensive not in that they endeavour to incorporate the full range of the authority's activities, but rather that they seek to identify all the corporate issues that the authority wishes to tackle concurrently, rather than sequentially. There are then three possible (and not mutually exclusive) avenues of implementation:

   - developing specific initiatives (or programmes) in response to each strategic priority and allocating resources to them;

   - requiring each service department to take into account the corporate agenda by demonstrating the relevance of existing activities, or developing new initiatives which address the strategic agenda;

   - using the strategy as a means of generating additional income (e.g. via a Single Regeneration Budget (SRB) or lottery bid) and/or persuading other agencies to take action (and allocate resources) in accordance with one or more of the strategic priorities.

2. *Topic-specific approaches*: These involve a more gradual, opportunistic approach to corporate strategy. Strategic priorities are identified individually, as and when a local authority identifies a specific issue or opportunity (e.g. the closure of a large local firm results in the perceived need for a strategic economic regeneration initiative). The 'de facto' corporate strategy then becomes the cumulative list of strategic initiatives which have over time been identified and followed up in this way. Again the three alternative but not mutually exclusive avenues of implementation apply.

3. *Service-based approaches*: In this case, the corporate strategy is what emerges from a process of prioritising existing services, and allocating resources in response to that process of priorisation. The process may be structured around service strategies which are then used as 'bid documents', and may define services in conventional departmental terms (e.g. social services, education) or, more usefully, in relation to more specific areas (services for children, the elderly, the disabled etc within social services).

This approach can be viewed as a corporate strategy only in so far as it involves informed comparison between and prioritisation of existing services. It does not address a corporate agenda which transcends existing service categories.

Conclusion

In one sense the different elements of corporate strategy identified can be seen as a menu, from which local authorities will select or ignore items depending upon their preference and circumstances. A comparison between the strategic documents which we have collected in connection with this book confirms that this selection process does indeed take place. Some authorities provided strategies which are in effect mission statements (i.e. statements of core values), others emphasise priorities for action and pay little attention to core values. Some authorities provide strategies which are in effect summaries of priorities from service strategies, sometimes including some form of inter-service prioritisation process. In some documents the role and purpose of activities are highlighted: in others this agenda is not directly addressed.

In Chapters 7 and 8 we explore in more detail the options, good practice and pitfalls in relation to core values/mission statements and strategic visions respectively, recognising that what is possible in each case will depend upon the political composition and culture of the authority concerned.

SUMMARY

- Strategic planning and management are concerned with identifying and responding to the various choices facing local authorities. Six types of choice can be identified:

    (i)   choices to prioritise organisational resources to *objectives* of perceived significance (typically but not necessarily non-service-specific);

    (ii)   choices between alternative *means* (or policies) for achieving such objectives;

    (iii) choices of priority *between* such objectives when a conflict or mismatch becomes apparent;

    (iv)   choices of which *cultural attributes* the authority wishes to adopt and express;

    (v)   choices made in response to an *unanticipated crisis* or *externally generated* pressure for action;

    (vi)   choices of organisational action as initiative in pursuit of items (i)–(v).

    Of these choices (i)–(iv) can be reasonably tackled in a proactive and planned way, and are hence appropriate topics for a strategic planning process. Choices (v) and (vi) are necessarily more reactive in nature and form the basis of strategic management.

- The following distinctions may helpfully be made between different types and levels of strategic initiative:

    (i)   strategic planning and strategic management (see above);

    (ii)   strategic choices about:

        – role and purpose;

        – authority-wide priorities for action;

        – particular services;

    (iii) authority-wide priorities for action may involve:

        – core values/mission statements;

        – agendas of substantive strategic issues/strategic vision;

  – strategic responses to unanticipated issues;

(iv) approaches to corporate strategy can be:

  – comprehensive;

  – topic-specific;

  – service-based.

■ Strategic documents and plans do not in themselves constitute strategic management. They may or may not be useful instruments for strategic management, but should not be equated with it.

4

The development of strategic planning and management

INTRODUCTION

In this chapter we examine the origins and development of corporate strategic management in general, and its development in the particular context of British local government. Consideration is given to:

- the evolution of *thinking* surrounding strategic management;

- the evolution of *practice* – the ways in which local authorities over the years have geared up to become more strategic.

The first section considers the development of what might be called the 'corporate dimension' in local government, the organisational changes over the years which have produced a relatively low level of corporate cohesion within local authorities and conditioned a receptiveness towards corporate management methods. The second section explores the development of management thinking and the impact of ideas about the nature and importance of corporate strategy upon local councils.

Evolution of the corporate dimension in local government

The need for corporate management and planning in local government can only be understood with reference to the evolving structure of local authorities and the weak 'corporate dimension' of their organisation. The roles and responsibilities of local authorities expanded rapidly from the 1850s.

A range of new services were provided and for each new service a new specialist board or committee was formed. As the number of boards increased, however, this fragmented structure became increasingly problematic, with citizens subject in some places to 18 separate rates. Eventually it was recognised that these fragments needed to be pulled together into a whole, and between 1872 and 1902 the system of local governance was rationalised by merging boards into 'compendious' authorities, unified councils from which specific committees derived their authority (Finer 1950, p.22). However, these pre-existing committees retained considerable power and independence within a pluralistic local authority, and hence the problem of co-ordination was not really solved but internalised. During the nineteenth century there were powerful mayors in some cities, such as Joseph Chamberlain in Birmingham, and yet 'statutes gave no encouragement to dynamic political leadership, as in the "strong mayor" concept found in the United States, as in the strong administrative leadership through the city managers' (Keith-Lucas and Richards 1978, p.17). At the turn of the century it was argued that a legal specialist should be appointed to councils leaving the town clerk free to provide overall supervision (Waller 1983, p.285). However professionalisation added a third pluralistic dimension to local authority organisation and culture, as each new service was associated with the emergence of a new municipal profession. Departments were created around the nucleus provided by these professions and adopted a form of administrative practice which reflected these origins.

Central government funding and supervision of local services increased especially from the 1870s, and grants-in-aid were tied to particular services, not provided to the authority as a whole. The corporate existence of local authorities was acknowledged in the new block grant of 1929, but earmarked funds remained the predominant form of grants-in-aid. Government inspectors were appointed to monitor the quality of local authority services, but standards were imposed separately for each service and thereby reinforced their compartmentalisation. The increasing penetration of party politics into local government during the interwar period, although it eroded the already weak position of the mayor, also went some way towards improving internal co-ordination. The offices of 'leader of the council' and 'leader of the opposition' were introduced, together with a committee of principal chairs of committees, by the Labour party in London during the 1930s (Wheare 1955, p.200). But the scope and professionalisation of local authority services continued to increase and to reinforce the pluralistic structure. Indeed delegation to committees was strengthened under the Local Authorities Act 1933, which gave these 'the full power of executive action' (Redlich and Hirst 1970, p.234).

The plea for greater co-ordination was taken up again in the post war period. In 1949 a committee of local authority associations recommended that the town clerk should become the chief executive officer of the council. It was suggested that an Establishment and General Administrative Committee be formed to take a comprehensive view of the civic machine (Smellie 1968, p.95). But central supervision and the professionalisation of services were increasing within the emerging welfare state, reinforcing the fragmentary tendencies (Wraith 1966, p.132). Partly in response to this, policy and resources committees were introduced in many councils during the 1960s to strengthen co-ordination (Bedford had a Management Committee, Basildon had a 'Committee of Chairmen'). Sir John Maud in 1966 recommended the streamlining of council organisations, and authorities in Liverpool, Newcastle, West Bromwich, Bedford, Grimsby, Ealing, and Camden experimented with the grouping together of departments, fewer committees, and a new kind of chief officer (Maud 1966, p.495). In 1967 the Maud Committee on local government reported that there was too much dispersal of control within local councils, with too many members and committees. The reports of Redcliffe-Maud (1969) and Bains (1972) advocated that a corporate approach be established by an overall manager. Gradually from the late 1960s, and more quickly after reorganisation in 1973/74, the town clerk was replaced by the chief executive. But despite acknowledgements of the 'corporate deficit' in reviews of local government during the 1950s and 60s, the committee system was largely unchanged under re-organisation in 1972 and the powers of delegation to committees were further increased without any corresponding legislative steps to strengthen political or managerial leadership. Corporate ambitions returned to centre stage from the early 1980s, first in a range of substantive policy initiatives (towards equal opportunities or economic development), and then towards a concern with formal management procedures. One of the few growth areas in local government between 1988 and 1992 was corporate strategic management, with the proliferation of central policy units, policy planning and review processes, and total quality management initiatives.

From the nineteenth century onwards the history of local government reveals two opposed organisational tendencies. It reveals a strong and persistent tendency towards the entrenchment of a pluralistic, decentred organisational structure based upon committees and departments, and reinforced by professionalism, the weakness of the centre, and by the pattern of central government funding and supervision. Once in place the committee system became self-reinforcing, inducing shared interests between departmental officers and committee members, and between local and central government, which militated against change. Alongside this persistent reality, however, has

31

run a recurrent and growing reaction against pluralism – against the inconsistency and compartmentalisation of local services – and towards the re-integration of activities within a single unified structure and policy framework. The drive towards corporate management systems, like the replacement of town clerks by chief executives, was one of several steps that have been taken over the years to improve the co-ordination and corporate cohesion of local councils. Recently the Heseltine review of local government organisation put forward proposals which would allow local authorities to devise structures and approaches which could strengthen the capacity for strategy and co-ordination. But so far the implementation of these initiatives has been slow and the legislation has not been enacted. To a considerable extent the future of local authority corporate cohesion is currently hanging in the balance, and depends upon the way government locally and nationally responds to the challenge posed by the proliferation of quangos and by the growth of competition (Collinge 1997).

Management thought and corporate strategy

Ideas about corporate strategy in and beyond the management literature do not exist in isolation, but are bound up with a number of cross-cutting intellectual and practical strands of thought. In this section we consider the development of ideas about corporate strategy, and examine their evolution especially in relation to the public sector and local government.

Histories of management thought generally begin with Max Weber, the German sociologist who was preoccupied with the growth of bureaucracy in the late nineteenth and early twentieth century, especially in the administration of the modern state. Or they begin with Frederick W. Taylor, the American engineer who developed 'scientific management', applying the methods of mechanical engineering to the design of manual tasks in the large, mechanised manufacturing plants that were emerging around the turn of the century. The sociological approach was developed throughout the 1950s and 60s, examining business and governmental organisations as complex social units embedded in a wider society. This process was associated with the growth of 'systems theory' (under the influence of Talcott Parsons and Robert Merton) as a way of accounting for organisational behaviour in terms of the values of participants, and their impact upon the internal and external relationships of the organisation. It was also associated during the 1960s and 70s with 'conflict theories' which stressed that different groups have different interests and powers stemming from their position in the organisation and in the wider society, and pursue these interests in opposition to one another (such as Crozier 1964; Hyman 1972). Industrial and organisational conflicts are interpreted by some commentators as a reflection of the development of opposing strategies, and of resistance to these strategies, amongst managers and workers of different grades. More recently there has been a tendency at least in some quarters for larger organisations to be fragmented by the contracting out of services and the incorporation of the market forces ('the internal market'). This, together with a new emphasis upon strategic alliances between companies, has produced an intellectual response in the shift of attention towards theories of markets and networks as alternative ways of achieving social co-ordination alongside organisational hierarchies (Thompson *et al* 1991).

While a sociological branch of organisational theory was emerging which stressed the role of values in organisational behaviour, another strand of management theory took economics as its starting point and was attempting to flesh out the economic model of business behaviour by studying management decision making. Economists generally assume that economic decisions are fully rational, that they are based on possession of full information about the organisation and its environment, and a full appreciation of the options which are available. However in reality managers are constrained by the complexity of the choices they face, the difficulty of the calculations involved and the relative absence of useful information, not to mention their irrational impulses, group attachments and loyalties. One strand of organisational theory which emerged in the 1950s was therefore related to the 'behavioural' theory of the firm and its willingness to give greater recognition to the realities of management. Particular stress was placed upon the understanding of practical decision making and, on this basis, assisting in the design of decision procedures in large firms (Simon 1957; Cyert and March 1963). Cyert and March came to the view that organisations are coalitions of groups with different interests, and acknowledged that these may each be pursuing their own goals which may conflict with one another, and which may be negotiated through a process of bargaining. The quality of the decisions that are taken will be revealed through the outcome that is achieved and the results will feed back to influence future decision-making through an adaptive, learning process.

Operational research was the name given to the analysis of decision-making as this emerged during World War II in the context of military planning. It has been defined as 'the attack of modern science on problems of decision-making arising in the management of operations' (Friend and Jessop 1969, p. xx), and involves 'dynamic programming', 'optimisation theory', 'critical path analysis', cost benefit analysis, systems analysis, control engineering and the computer modelling of decisions. Likewise the concept of 'strategy' originated in a military context, was given a higher profile especially during World War II, and led to an emphasis upon ways of bolstering the rationality of corporate decisions. The rationalistic approach to corporate planning and business strategy reached its high point in the 1960s. This approach was associated with the post-war growth of big business and big government and was reflected through matters as varied as defence and macro-economic policy, industry and employment, national and regional development, land use and urban design, service programming and budget setting (Collinge 1996). To varying degrees it was assumed in each of these contexts that the tools of logical analysis could be used to determine the optimal design of corporate decision processes. Igor Ansoff, for example, sought to apply analytical methods and systems theory to solving 'the total strategic problem of the firm' (Ansoff 1965, p.vii). Ansoff's stress was upon decision making, viewing business strategy formation as 'the cornerstone of successful management' (Ansoff 1965, p.vii). He examined the components of strategy in order to conceptualise the firm's business, and the results of his analysis often took the form of complex designs for the management of 'decision flows', combined with orderly models of the hierarchical relationship between strategies and plans at different levels of the organisation (Ansoff 1965, pp.202–203, p.225).

These themes were also reflected to varying degrees in local authority management. The techniques of operational research were advocated for application to local authority services during the 1960s by the Tavistock Institute of Human Relations and the Institute for Operational Research. It was argued in 1969 that planning processes must be developed in local – and national – government which utilise methods which constitute a 'technology of strategic choice', and that new organisational forms will be required to support these techniques and processes (Friend and Jessop 1969, p.xx). The emphasis is upon planning which encompasses not only land use and physical development but also finance and manpower as well as specific services (mainly transport, education and housing). However attention tended in practice to focus down upon physical planning and resource planning, as perhaps more tangible and quantifiable issues more amenable to the operational management approach than the others (e.g. Friend and Jessop 1969, p.46). Managers in the public sector were much influenced, for instance, by the Planning, Programming and Budgeting Systems (PPBS) approach adopted first in the US military. On the other hand, the expansion of local government during the 1960s and the growth of cross-departmental issues and responsibilities lead to increased focus upon corporate management as this had developed in the private sector. This was reflected in the discussions of the Maud and Bains Committees, and the establishment by some councils of policy and resources committees, the appointment of a chief executive, and increased use of budget planning. When local government was reorganised in 1973/74 the new upper tier in the large conurbations (metropolitan counties) was seen as responsible for 'strategic issues' such as structure planning and passenger transport. Corporate planning practices introduced at this time in particular tended to stress the formalisation of procedures, and the central preparation of documents and manuals that were to be followed in a rather rigid manner.

Critique and renewal

During the 1970s, however, many of these ideas and the assumptions concerning corporate management were thrown into doubt by events internal and external to the organisation. Complex corporate planning procedures and documents seemed increasingly out of touch with the practical realities of organisations, and were too inflexible to respond to an increasingly rapid and uneven rate of change. The growing mood of disenchantment was captured particularly well in the writings of Aaron Wildavsky. Wildavsky ruminated throughout the 1960s and 1970s upon the meaning of 'planning' in economic and land-use as well as management and government settings, and argued that professional planners have found it more difficult than they expected to control the future. Indeed there may be no 'general will' that can be embodied in a single plan, but competing wills in conflict around and within one or more plans (Wildavsky 1973, p.140). According to Wildavsky, the PPBS approach is irrational because it attempted to link all budget and service decisions together in a process that leads to paralysis. Planning is considered virtuous whatever its practical value because it embodies universal norms of rational choice, but the rational requirements of different parts of the organisation may directly conflict with one another. Wildavsky concludes that 'planning stands for unresolved conflicts' (Wildavsky 1973, p.146). Corporate planning procedures as applied in British government were also criticised from another angle, for attempting to displace the

> **Corporate planning procedures were criticised for attempting to displace the political control of councils by introducing a managerial culture.**

political control of councils by introducing a managerial or business culture which applies the technocratic gospel of corporate management to the solution of political problems that have been reinterpreted as 'administrative', while at the same time smuggling the technocrats' own political values into the heart of the organisation (Benington 1976, p.15, p.19; Cockburn 1977).

Despite practical and political difficulties encountered by corporate planning and indeed by national planning during the 1960s and 70s, there was a renewed emphasis upon 'strategy' in local government from the late 1970s and into the early 1980s. But strategies were now seen – at least in the highly charged political atmosphere of the larger urban authorities – as primarily a political statement building upon the ruling party manifesto. Many British local authorities, for example, adopted 'economic strategies', 'industrial strategies', 'training strategies' and 'anti-poverty strategies' to express their political commitments in opposition to the Conservative government of Margaret Thatcher. On the other hand, the prestige of corporate strategic management was being renewed in a business context through the expansion of business schools offering MBA programmes containing courses on 'business policy', and the impact of books such as *In Search of Excellence* by Peters and Waterman (1982), *Explorations in Corporate Strategy* by Johnson and Scholes (1988) and *The Strategy Process* by Mintzberg (1991). These kinds of texts, whether or not they are always strictly applicable, struck a chord with managers beyond the private sector, and were widely consulted in local government.

The pressure on local authority discretion in services and budgets from the mid-1980s has induced many councils once again to adopt a strategic approach to corporate management, and to introduce formalised policy planning processes (Collinge and Leach 1995). The Audit Commission argued in the late 1980s that, for instance, while systematic forward planning had been somewhat discredited, any council wishing to shape its future must operate a simple but effective policy planning system (Audit Commission 1988, p.10). It was seen as critical that local authorities have robust mechanisms for reaching corporate decisions, and that the chief executive has a responsibility for ensuring that there is 'strategic planning' in councils, and for converting policy into strategy (Audit Commission 1989, p.2).

Elected members were exhorted by the Audit Commission to set policy and to represent their areas, but to avoid detailed interference in day-to-day operational management. In many areas, contracting out will make this virtually impossible anyway (Audit Commission 1988, p.9).

As these ideas caught hold, however, we saw once again a recurrence of the dangers of a mechanistic approach to strategy making, in which policy planning specialists attempt to produce detailed plans for activities they cannot control, or are left to produce statements of organisational values that are so bland they are meaningless. There appears once again to be a dual danger at least in the public sector of, on the one hand, excessive zeal in applying a rationalistic notion of strategic management which provokes another backlash from managers and politicians, and on the other hand of rejecting the notion of strategy altogether and reverting to an ad hoc method of management based upon 'muddling through'. It is therefore important to achieve a balanced understanding of strategy, of its significance and of its limitations, and in particular to find a way of moving beyond a rationalistic planning approach.

It is in this context that we can refer to Henry Mintzberg's examination of the ascent and decline of strategic planning from the 1950s to the present day (Mintzberg 1994). The focus of Mintzberg's attention is upon planning in the private sector, upon planning as one route to strategy, and upon strategy as a component of planning. His professed objective is to point out the deficiencies of much that has been written about strategic planning in order to recover what remains of value in this concept. Many of his observations have a direct bearing upon the approach to management problems that is sometimes adopted in local authorities. Mintzberg analyses the assumptions underlying strategic planning and identifies four of these: the assumption of detachment, quantification, pre-determination, and formalisation.

The first assumption – that of *detachment* – describes the divorce of strategic management from operational management, the division between the formulation of strategy and its execution. It is all too often assumed that the preparation of the strategy must be delegated to a specialist team, and there is a danger that this team will become detached from the process of service delivery and so of implementation. But Mintzberg suggests that effective strategists are not people who abstract themselves from daily concerns, but 'the ones who immerse themselves in it while being able to abstract the strategic messages from it' (Mintzberg 1994, p.256).

For the assumption of detachment to work there must be a way of supplying information to managers aside from day-to-day contact, and this method is conceived in the management literature as formal, quantitative management information systems – involving the fallacy of *quantification*. Hard, quantitative information (such as numerical performance indicators) tends to drive out qualitative impressions, such as the mood of people and their morale, which are of crucial importance in strategic decision making. Much information that managers require is not only soft and difficult to communicate to anybody not in the swim, but also implicit even to the managers themselves. It follows that managers who are in the know, with hands-on control over departments, should take active charge of the strategy-making process and use their intuition to reach decisions rather than rely upon external specialist planners: 'Effective strategy-making under difficult circumstances requires either that the formulator be the implementor or else that the implementors take personal charge of the formulation' (Mintzberg 1994 p.273). These observations seem to contradict the current emphasis upon 'steering' rather than 'rowing', and the desire to exclude elected members from detailed involvement in services (Audit Commission 1988; Osborne and Gaebler 1992; Mintzberg 1994, p.272; for a critique see Stewart 1996).

The assumption of *pre-determination* is to be found in the assumed ability of managers to forecast the environment, the ability to unfold the strategy on demand, and to implement it according to a clear programme (Mintzberg 1994, pp.227–8). However forecasting, especially of discontinuities, is notoriously difficult and usually only succeeds in extrapolating from the present.

Mintzberg's last assumption is that of *formalisation* and rests on the premise that strategies must be developed through a carefully programmed process of information gathering, review, decision and implementation. The problem with formalisation is that it breaks activities down into their component parts and stresses analysis as the way of strategy making. But creativity cannot be programmed through stages on a check-list in the way that Taylor tried to programme mechanical tasks: 'the work of creating strategy cannot be programmed like that of shovelling coal' (Mintzberg 1994, p.303). Mintzberg reminds us that while the left hemisphere of the brain seems to be associated with language, logic and systematic thought, the right side seems to specialise in spatial perception, emotion, relational thinking and synthesis. While most management is about using the right, creative and synthesising side of the brain, planning tends to emphasise the left, analytical, and rationalistic side. But both are required for a planning team, although the balance between them will depend upon the type of organisation concerned.

Mintzberg argues that three approaches to strategy formation must be combined within organisations: planning; visionary; and learning. His main point is simply to combat the supposed over-emphasis on planning as a way of creating strategy. The 'visionary' approach aims to set broad outlines for a strategy while leaving the details to be specified in practice, allowing more room for responding flexibly to unexpected events. The 'learning' approach allows ideas to emerge within the organisation and to be taken on through adaptation where the ideas are beneficial. The 'planning' approach is emphasised because it give a sense of security, both to those inside the organisation, and to important other bodies on which the organisation depends. In a local authority context, for example, learning will take place by policy-makers and managers listening to the views of citizens, customers and staff, and encouraging these to comment on how services can be improved.

The separation of thinking and acting in the planning model of strategy tends to propagate a top-down approach to strategy formation. It creates a disposition against finding out from lower levels of the organisation ideas and constraints that might produce a better and more well supported corporate strategy: 'Instead of the formulation-implementation dichotomy so long promoted in the prescriptive literature, we believe the strategy-making process is best characterised as a process of learning ... people act in order to think, and they think in order to act' (Mintzberg 1994, p.286). A grass roots model of strategy formation may emerge, with individuals, sections and divisions devising or copying good ways of doing things, and emergent strategies are moulded through conscious deliberation until they are embraced selectively by senior management.

In drawing attention to the limitations of the planning approach and the pursuit of what – following Ansoff – might be called 'total strategy', Mintzberg risks pushing us towards the opposite extreme of 'no strategy'. Aware of this danger he argues towards the end of his book that in drawing the reader away from the planning model he has had to overstate his case. Strategy formation is now seen as requiring both the analysing skills of the planner and the synthesising skills of the manager, and planning should be seen as support for strategy formation rather than as a substitute for it. The legitimate roles of planning are three-fold: identifying the organisation's emergent strategies; analysing hard data and presenting this to senior managers; and drawing attention to future issues and future thinking in the broadest sense. 'In the catalyst role ... the planner does not enter the black box of strategy making so much as ensure that the box is occupied with active line manager' (Mintzberg 1994, p.382).

Over recent years there has been an attempt to rethink the approach to corporate strategy, to avoid the rigidities of a mechanistic approach without falling prey to the opposite danger of having no strategic approach. Sotarauta has attempted to address these changes by building upon Mintzberg in developing an alternative to these classical view of strategy and strategic management (Sotarauta 1995). He stresses the importance of the processual and systemic nature of strategy, and the intimate connection between formulation and implementation that arises when strategies are developed in midstream, as is generally the case in practice.

While the classical way of viewing strategies as designed, rational plans for implementation, may be applicable in some situations, more generally the process-orientated 'soft strategy' concept will be more useful. The essential features of soft strategies are simplicity, asymmetry and perishability. The *simplicity* of soft strategies lies in their emphasis upon a few leading bright ideas. The *asymmetry* of these strategies lies in their generality and their consistency with a variety of different and fragmentary strategies in the constituent sections of councils. The *perishability* of strategies refers to their incomplete and evanescent character. Sotarauta points out that the first step in strategy development should be to identify those strategies that have actually been implemented up to now. These represent the input into the new design process which produces an intended course of action, a guideline to deal with future contingencies. It is possible for intended strategies to fail, to be sidelined and not implemented, and this will lead to a process of learning whereby the intended strategy is modified. It is also possible for intended strategies to be displaced by emergent strategies, by activities and organisational dispositions which grow out of the multiplicity of activities which are undertaken. Sotarauta concludes that strategies develop constantly and may never be realised, but may exist as 'virtual' conditions to which the organisation aspires and which guides its behaviour.

For Sotarauta the soft strategy is informed by a strategic consciousness, or a vision which holds managers to a particular path and shapes their activities even in response to contingencies. Strategic consciousness is a way of achieving long-range consistency within the milieu of short-term decision-making and events. A strategy should be seen not as a plan but as a mirror, a way of seeing and evaluating events and the responses which the organisation must make

> A strategy should be seen not as a plan but as a mirror, a way of seeing and evaluating events.

to these. Where these responses are necessary but inconsistent with the agreed strategy then they may proceed anyway, and the strategy will either be retained in a diluted form or perhaps questioned.

SUMMARY

Considering the development of the 'corporate dimension' of local authorities in the UK, and the development of management ideas concerning corporate strategy formation, it is possible to draw out some key conclusions and points of reference for practitioners.

■ Strategic management in local government is caught up in the tension between two opposite tendencies, towards the reinforcement of a decentralised organisational structure based upon the committee system, and towards the forging of corporate cohesion and the co-ordination of these committees from the corporate centre.

- Ideas concerning corporate strategic management, ideas which are extant within local authorities and amongst consultant and researchers, derive both from the concerns of practitioners, and from strands of theoretical writing which include organisational analysis. They are subject to the vagaries of intellectual fashions and should be treated with a degree of caution.

- There is a tendency for certain corporate managers (including some within local government) to favour more rationalistic, mechanistic approaches to the development of corporate strategy. However, experience suggests that these approaches presuppose a degree of knowledge and power that no single person or team can or should possess.

- On the other hand, there is also a tendency for corporate managers that have been adversely affected by the consequences of the mechanistic approach to reject the whole notion of strategic management and to revert back to a form of muddling through. This is an equal but opposite error, throwing the proverbial baby out with the bath water.

- Between these extremes lie various new approaches to the understanding of corporate management, approaches which stress the combination of 'top down' and 'bottom up', 'designed' and 'emergent' strategy formation processes, and which emphasise organisational learning and the need for pliant or 'soft' strategies.

5

The organisational context of local authority strategies

INTRODUCTION

Until recently, the dominant basis of organisation in the majority of local authorities has been the 'department', normally though not always defined around a particular professional skill, or set of related skills (*see* Leach, Stewart and Walsh, 1994, Chapter 2). Typically there has also been a link between a 'department' of this nature and a 'committee' whose remit mirrored that of the department, a link which often resulted in a close mutually supportive relationship between chief officer and committee chair. Such departments and committees often operated in a relatively detached way from the rest of the authority. Consider for example, the degree of autonomy associated with education departments and committees in the shire counties, before the local authority role in education was destabilised by the provision of the 1988 Education Act. Traditionally, police, highways and housing have often operated in a similar detached way.

Relationships between such service-providing departments and the local authority's centre could be characterised by two features: the desire on the part of the service department to maximise its resource allocation within the authority's budget process, and its desire to enjoy as much autonomy (or discretion) as possible from central 'interference'. Terms such as 'warring baronies' and 'independent fiefdoms' were coined to characterise such productivity. The introduction of 'corporate planning' in the 1970s, was viewed widely by such departments and committees as a centrally inspired potential threat to their own autonomy/discretion and was thought to have potentially destabilising implications for future resource allocations. In short, rather than welcomed, corporate planning was invariably viewed with suspicion.

The strength of the profession-based service department/committee system in the workings of local authorities has been challenged and often weakened by a whole range of recent changes: the devolvement of managerial and financial to 'unit managers'; the organisational separation of client and contractor's role; the introduction of multi-service directorates; and the explicit requirements placed on management team members to operate on a corporate strategic basis. However it would be premature to argue that linked departments and committees have ceased to be significant sub-units within local authorities. Firstly, many councils have chosen not to adopt a directorate system. Secondly, in those authorities which have adopted such a system, there are plenty of examples of directorates which operate as super-departments, concerned predominantly with the range of services within their remit, and very little with any wider corporate agenda. In some cases, the directorate system amounts to little more than a thin organisational veneer with a traditional departmental system hiding behind it. The political status of committee chairs remains high in most authorities, ensuring that senior members will continue to fight the corner of their particular service committee. Indeed most council budgets are still drawn up and scrutinised on a committee by committee basis. Thus although the dominance of resource battles between different service committees/departments and battles over autonomy between such committees/departments and the centre have been diluted in the culture of local authorities by a range of recent changes, such processes are still, in most authorities, a significant force; and service departments (or directorates) still often view corporate strategies as a threat for the same kind of reasons that corporate planning in the 1970s was so viewed.

Theoretical underpinnings

This impressionistic account of the nature and power of departmentalism as a phenomenon, is congruent with the perspectives and findings of a number of influential writers on the behaviour of public sector organisations. Benson (1975) argues that such organisations are orientated towards the procurement and enhancement of two key resources – money and authority. Wildavsky (1975; 1979) demonstrates how a range of tactics are deployed by such agencies to protect existing budgets, arguing for growth or against cuts. Niskanen (1971) argues that the head of public agencies strive to maximise agency budgets, on the basis of personal motivation, 'because larger budgets push up salaries and fringe benefits, enhance status and build up organisational slack'. Dunleavy (1991) challenges Niskanen's view of the motivations of bureau heads and argues that the concept of 'bureau shaping' is a more powerful explanatory tool. Heads of bureau seek a balance between rewarding work and resources, and may be prepared to see relatively routine elements of these responsibilities transferred elsewhere, if the outcome is a more rewarding set of bureau tasks.

All of the above writers were studying single purpose public agencies operating at a national level, and bargaining situations in which the key protagonists were officials rather than politicians. The situation within local authorities is more complex, in that they are multi-purpose rather than single purpose agencies. The bargaining process is an internal one rather than one which involves the preparation of a case to an external agency. Nonetheless, there is ample evidence from those who have studied budgetary processes in British local authorities (Greenwood 1983; Elcock and Jordan 1987; Elcock, Jordan and Midwinter 1989) that the behaviour of discrete organisational units within a local authority is not dissimilar in principle to the behaviour of 'single purpose' public agencies of the kind studies by Benson, Niskanen, Dunleavy and Wildavsky. This then is the organisational context and culture within which new strategic initiatives have to establish themselves, or in which established strategic initiatives have to survive or avoid being marginalised. But in arguing against such initiatives, arguments cannot overtly be made in terms of threats to the autonomy, interests or budgetary allocation of departments or committees. Strategic planning, as

> **Arguments against strategic planning have to be couched in terms of the interests of the authority, not its individual departments.**

we noted in Chapter 2 sounds in principle a sensible and desirable activity. Arguments against its introduction have to be couched in terms of the interests of the authority itself, not the individual departments and committees.

Arguments against corporate strategies

There are in fact a range of potential arguments against the relevance of corporate strategies which will be used by members or officers in the organisation who either believe them *per se*, or who use them as a legitimisation for concerns about ways in which the strategy may affect their freedom of manoeuvre or resource position within the authority.

The main arguments against the development of a corporate strategy which identifies authority-wide priorities for action (as opposed to corporate values) are as follows.

1. It is not an appropriate role – the emphasis should be on services.

2. It may be an appropriate role in principle but it can't be afforded in the present hard financial times.

3. It is politically implausible – the setting of long-term objectives makes more difficult the need for political 'short-termism' and manoeuvring that comes to the fore in particular before elections.

The appropriateness of corporate strategy

The first objection takes us back to the discussion of role and purpose in Chapter 2. It is a perfectly tenable value position to hold that a local authority should see its dominant role as service provision. It is a role definition which carries with it certain dangers, not least when faced with a central government ideologically predisposed to move local services to other agencies. However, it is a philosophy with long tradition within local government, and if that is what the controlling group wishes to adopt then that is a legitimate political choice.

If the service provision role is emphasised, then strategic planning does not become unnecessary but it does take on a different and more limited form. The arguments for mission statements and core values and the task of translating these into action are as relevant for such authorities as for those who wish to pursue more ambitious strategic agendas. What does become unnecessary, by definition, is a corporate agenda which addresses wider issues which transcend service provision. Two arguments for a substantive corporate strategy remain.

1. The case for identifying areas of inter-service co-ordination where the overall impact of service provision can be improved (or rendered more cost-effective) by co-ordinative action.

2. The need for prioritisation amongst different services and in particular amongst services which are not mandatory (or where the level of service provision is not specified) to aid the resource allocation process.

Strategy and financial constraint

The two strategic desiderata noted above are equally relevant for an authority which favours a community governance approach. But in that case, there is an additional task – that of identifying and prioritising those wider issues on which the authority wishes to take action.

The second counter-argument: 'we can't afford it in the present financial climate' is an argument of contingency rather than of principle. Corporate strategies addressing a wide range of community problems may be a good idea but not, it is argued, at a time when it is proving increasingly difficult to finance basic services. The introduction of a more ambitious corporate strategic initiative is dependent, from this perspective, on such changes as the removal of universal council tax capping, the return of NNDR to local government, the relaxation of current capital controls and a less stringent RSG settlement. There are several ways in which this argument can be challenged.

1. Although the Labour government may well act positively in relation to the first three of these financial constraints, it is unlikely to do so in the fourth. The importance of keeping down the Public Sector Borrowing Requirement (PSBR) in the context of the growing internationalisation of capital flows and markets, makes it highly unlikely that a future government of any political persuasion will permit more than marginal increases in Rate Support Grant (RSG). Thus at best there will be some marginal improvement in the scope for financial manoeuvre and choice in local authorities (the return of National Non-domestic Rates (NNDR), for example,would reduce the impact of the gearing effect of increased expenditure on council tax increases). But the 'resource scarcity' argument is unlikely to disappear. However, the exhortation to respond to a wide range of social economic and environmental needs within the authority's area would be likely to become a significant feature of a Labour government's programme for local government thus intensifying the perceived mismatch between resource availability and the development of wide-ranging corporate strategies.

2. It can be argued that it is erroneous to equate action in pursuit of a corporate strategic agenda with the expenditure of financial resources. It is true that the pursuit of a strategic priority is likely to have some expenditure implications but there are a variety of other ways in which strategic objectives can be furthered which involve modes of local authority action with marginal financial implications for the local authority. One of these corollaries of the idea of community governance is to tap resources from either organisations (e.g. private sector) or collectives (e.g. the local community). Stewart (1995a) has identified a number of different ways in which a strategic agenda can be taken forward.

    That may involve direct provision, but a local authority can regulate; can provide grants; can use its influence in the local economy as a major employer or major purchaser of goods; can assist others through the knowledge, skills and information it deploys; can bring together organisations, individuals and groups; can build or assist new organisations; can contract with other organisations for the provision of goods and services; can involve users in the running of services; can speak on behalf of its area and those who live within it.

3. The 'concentration on service responsibilities in a hard financial climate' argument assumes that all the services provided by a local authority – including those which are non-mandatory – will be found to be more important than all the new possibilities implied by a more wide-ranging strategic agenda. They may not be and there would be nothing to lose by putting the assumption to the test. The continuance of a subsidy to a declining, 'middle-of-the-road' local theatre may conceivably turn out to be of lower priority than a modest development in a range of measures to combat the incidence and fear of crime. By setting service provision priorities side-by-side with priorities desired from a broader scan of local needs and preferences, the strength of the argument for concentrating resources on existing services can explicitly be tested.

4. In so far as the pursuit of corporate strategic priorities involves the way in which things are done, rather than what is done, then implementation becomes possible, at least in part, through changes in the way services are specified, provided or distributed: a commitment to equal opportunities is likely to affect the distribution of many services, for example; a concern to boost the local economy may result in predisposition to purchase from local firms; whenever possible a commitment to environmental sustainability may be expressed in terms of a set of 'environmental quality' criteria to which local service providers must conform if the council is to continue to use their services or products. Indeed, as we argue in Chapter 9 one way in which a corporate strategy can be made to influence the budgetary process is to require service committees/departments to demonstrate that contribution of their revenue bids (or arguments against cuts) in terms of the corporate strategic priorities.

Strategy and political interest

The third objection – lack of congruence with political behaviour – is discussed in more detail in Chapter 6 (pp.54–5). There are indeed some potential political disadvantages associated with corporate strategies, notably the diminishment in the scope for political manoeuvring and resource allocation in the run-up to a local election. However, there are also significant political benefits: the more tangible expression of manifesto commitments; a clarification of political purpose; and the generation of public support. The reality in most authorities is that there will be a range of views amongst elected members about the value of a corporate strategy, with some likely to be supportive, others more critical, and the majority, initially at any rate, sceptical or indifferent. Once a strategic initiative gets under way, then political and managerial interests begin to interact, with member-officer alliances forming in support or opposition. The outcome of this situation will then depend on the dynamics of political/managerial power/influences relationships, and the skill with which tactics are displayed to support or marginalise the strategic initiative.

The implication of these arguments is that the development or continuation of a strategic initiative will always be subject to pressures for dilution or retraction, except in situations in which the strategy performs a predominantly symbolic function only in which case, of course, it is no real threat to anyone! That means that to succeed in changing the way decisions are made in a local authority a strategic initiative needs both organisational champions and appropriate organisational mechanisms to help establish it as a going concern.

> **The development of a strategic initiative will always be subject to pressures for dilution or retraction.**

Assessing strategic effectiveness

The recognition that the development or continuation of a strategic initiative will normally be subject to pressures for dilution or retraction leads to the question of in what circumstances can strategies be deemed to be 'effective' and how would we know? There are two relevant tests of the effectiveness, in organisational terms, of corporate strategies.

1. To what extent do they attract resources, cause resources to be diverted, and/or result in resource allocation in pursuit of the strategic priorities by external organisation.

2. To what extent do they influence the activities and behaviour of existing departments (e.g. by influencing a greater environmental awareness in existing service policies).

The first test applies to all three approaches to corporate strategy: the second only to the comprehensive and topic-specific approaches (*see* Chapter 3). It should be emphasised that what we are concerned with here is not the effectiveness of the policy initiatives developed in achieving strategic objectives but the effectiveness in organisational terms, as assessed by the attraction of resources and/or influences on existing activities.

Both criteria are in principle measurable. In relation to resource attraction, it can normally be ascertained the extent to which a strategic priority:

■ Involves an investment of *staff resources* (internally or externally) either through the establishment of a new position or unit with the authority's establishment, and/or the allocation of time to the strategic priority by existing staff;

■ involves *current expenditure* on the part of the local authority (or an external agency) in any one budgetary year and/or results in the attraction of external resources (e.g. lottery grants) that would not otherwise have been attracted;

■ involves *capital expenditure* either directly or indirectly (as above).

These resources are tangible and measurable. However, equally important though less tangible is the resource of support of people within the organisation. There are two elements here: the level of commitment/support amongst the majority party group or dominant coalition; and the level of commitment/support within the authority's management team. It could be argued that the level of organisational support will be manifested through the allocation of the more tangible resources of staff and financial expenditure. There will certainly be a relationship between the two influences, but in our view organisational support may in certain circumstances have an independent impact. If for example, a programme of action aimed at a strategic priority is having demonstrably little effect in the short term, then a high level or organisational commitment may help it survive, whereas a low level may result in its termination. Similarly a programme agreed as a relatively low priority strategic issue may, through subsequent demonstration of success, attract a higher level of political commitment which provides longer-term stability. In these ways organisational support may be a direct, as well as an indirect, criterion of the organisational effectiveness of a strategic priority.

The second type of criterion of organisational effectiveness – influence on existing programmes – would require a more in-depth study of change (or lack of change) in practice. But more superficially, an analysis of changes in departmental policy documents, allocation systems or contractual requirements and the prevalence of references to the strategic objective in committee reports would provide some evidence of the degree of influence.

One of the advantages of this framework is that it enables us to make comparisons within one authority of the effectiveness in organisational terms of either different strategic elements in a comprehensive corporate strategy, or the different topic-specific strategies which have been developed.

The roots of strategic effectiveness

It is important, however, to move beyond such comparisons of organisational effectiveness to an understanding of why some strategies are more effective in this sense, than others. We argued earlier that corporate strategies, of whatever description, are not usually developed or implemented within a supportive or even neutral organisational environment. Corporate strategies are frequently viewed by existing departmental interests and service committees as potential threats, as they are likely to compete for existing resources. If the budget of a leisure and recreation department begins to look increasingly vulnerable in relation to the resource demands of a new strategic priority relating, for example, to 'economic regeneration', then it is unlikely to elicit the enthusiastic support of either the director of leisure and recreation or the chair of the parallel committee. To put it another way, it would be expected, at the very least that each senior manager and committee chair would view the new strategic initiative from a service department/committee perspective. Does it provide opportunities to develop the department's programme of work or are there no such opportunities? In the latter case, the implication is that resources may be lost in the next budget round, to the new strategic initiative. All the studies of the behaviour of public bureaucracies, including the bureau shaping perspective of Dunleavy (1991) as well as the more traditional budget-maximisation perspective of Niskanen (1971) would support this kind of departmental interest-based analysis.

It follows that to understand, or predict the probabilities of a strategic objective or issue becoming effective (in the resource accumulation sense) one needs to know something of the organisational culture within which it develops. In particular it is crucial to understand:

1. Who are the *champions* of strategic initiative?

2. Who are its principal *opponents*?

3. What organisational *resources* (principally organisational position, status and political influence) do champions and opponents respectively possess?

4. How *effectively* do they deploy these resources tactically to further their beliefs and interest?

In initiating a strategic review such political and organisational sensitivity is crucial. Included below is a summary of the key points which should be borne in mind

---

Steps of a strategic review

Reviewing a corporate or cross-committee strategy

1. Determine on what authority the review is occurring.

2. Have close regard to the 'politics' of the process of review from the outset.

   ■ What are the purposes of the review, overt and covert?

   ■ Who has the power in the situation, and where is the tension?

   ■ Open channels of communication with all key power holders.

   ■ Establish and clarify the limits of your authority for yourself and with others.

3. Review the existing context before rushing to conclusions.

   ■ Consider existing information to support strategy.

   ■ Look at strategies that already exist – there may well be several.

   ■ Review communication channels (consultation, implementation) already in place.

   ■ Consider current co-ordinating mechanisms.

4. Take a pragmatic approach.

   ■ Use *existing* information.

   ■ Build upon *existing* strategies.

   ■ Identify *organisational pre-conditions* of a strategic approach: leadership at the right level; priorities; resources.

   ■ Identify *process* for establishing this.

The implication is that although some strategic initiatives may start from a more promising position than others (e.g. strong political support for an initiative will be particularly difficult to counter directly by opponents) there are very few cases that do not involve some kind of organisational contest between advocates and opponents, those who stand to gain and those who stand to lose.

SUMMARY

- An understanding of a local authority's organisational context and culture is crucial in planning how to introduce a strategic initiative and avoid it being marginalised;

- The main arguments used by opponents in the introduction of corporate strategies are as follows.

    (i)   The emphasis should be on improving or protecting services.

    (ii) It is an appropriate type of initiative but can't be afforded in the present hard financial climate.

    (iii) It is politically implausible, as it is not in councillors' interests to commit themselves to long-term goals.

- The form and content of corporate strategy depends on prior decisions about an authority's role and purpose. But even for authorities who wish to concentrate on service provision, there are two important roles for a corporate strategy:

    (i)   the need to identify and respond to problems requiring inter-service co-ordination;

    (ii) the need for privatisation between services to structure the resource allocation process.

- The Labour government's commitment to 'community plans' – which are a form of corporate strategy – is likely to increase the number of authorities adopting a 'community governance' role.

- It is erroneous to equate action in pursuit of a corporate strategy with the expenditure of financial resources. There are many other ways in which a strategic agenda can be taken forward, e.g. tapping community initiative, advocacy, leverage of finance from the agencies.

- It is always an open question whether all the services currently provided by a local authority (including non-mandatory service provision) will be found to be more important than initiatives implied by a corporate strategy.

- Many elements of corporate strategies are more concerned with the *way* things are done, rather than *what* is done, and hence do not necessarily involve new expenditure.

- There are three important tests of the effectiveness of a corporate strategy.

  (i) To what extent does it attract resources within the authority's budget process?

  (ii) To what extent does it influence the behaviour of existing departments?

  (iii) To what extent are corporate objectives actually achieved?

- In analysing the threats and opportunities facing a corporate strategy, the following check-list of questions is a helpful guide.

  (i) Who are the internal champions of the strategic initiative?

  (ii) Who are the principal opponents?

  (iii) What organisational resources (e.g. power, status, influence) do champions and opponents possess?

  (iv) How effectively are they deploying such resources?

6

The political context of strategic planning

INTRODUCTION

As we have already noted, strategic planning and management are by their very nature highly 'political' processes in two different senses.

- They imply the re-allocation of resources between different sub-divisions of the local authority (e.g. between departments, committees, local areas).

- They imply a recognition of party political priorities, and the development of such priorities into programmes of action.

To the second of these political dimensions there should, however, be added an important qualification. To the chief executive and other leading officers at the centre of a local authority, strategic planning is a management tool with many potential benefits and few drawbacks. Politicians are of course in a different position to officers. Consideration of electoral success may over-ride that of rational management, particularly as the 'next election' approaches. That is why it is not illogical, in political terms, for resources to be allocated prior to a local election in a way which seems inconsistent with strategic priorities. It may, for example be politically more important at such times to develop a higher profile in marginal wards rather than to follow the logic of a corporate strategy.

There is a second sense in which corporate strategies may work against political interests. A previous statement of aspirations or intentions may be referred back to with satisfaction if such aspirations are achieved, even if only partially. Such statements may, however, also act as hostages to fortune, in that they make the failure of achievement that much more obvious. Thus, although there are, as we have already argued, political advantages in explicit statements of corporate strategy, there are also dangers, which are a direct reflection of the electoral vulnerability of politicians (a vulnerability not shared by chief officers). Although it may be irrational managerially not to be explicit about intentions, it is not necessarily irrational politically. Political and managerial logic are by no means synonymous, as we have already argued. Thus, one would expect in any discussion about strategic planning, that politicians may wish to leave a greater scope for short-term manoeuvring and be less explicit about intentions (though no less ready to publicise achievements) than officers would be.

> Political and managerial logic are by no means synonymous ... politicians may wish to leave a greater scope for short-term manoeuvring.

This difference of perspective does not undermine the political cause for strategic planning; what it does do, is imply that the way it is publicly expressed may be an issue of considerable political sensitivity.

The politics of resource allocation

We looked at the impact of strategic planning on resources in the previous chapter and argued that 'organisational politics' is a phenomenon that has to be both understood, and taken account of if strategy is to become effective. Although the point was made in terms of organisational politics it is, in a sense, a 'party' political point also, in that typically in local authorities, the departmental system is paralleled by a committee system, through which heads of department and committee chairs develop common interests and powerful alliances. Thus, the threat posed by a corporate strategy to a departmental budget is invariably perceived as a threat also by the chair of the related service committee.

The input of political priorities

The second sense in which strategy is political – the expression of political priorities – does not necessarily imply a politically-led process of development although it may do so. The first draft of a strategy may be drawn up by a chief executive and presented to the council (or majority group) for its consideration. Indeed, if an authority is dominated by independents, or operates with a relatively low degree of formal politicisation (e.g. little emphasis on group discipline) or is hung (or balanced) with no two

55

parties forming either an up-front or 'behind the scenes' coalition, then it is likely that any strategic initiative will require an initiative of this nature from the chief executive. In doing so, however, a chief executive is only likely to be successful if he or she can identify the likely areas of political agreement (or majority support). The same point applies if the chief executive takes the strategic initiative in a situation where one party has a majority.

What is undoubtedly true is that if a strategic agenda or plan does not connect with, and in some sense reflect the priorities and ways of working of majority parties, co-operating parties in a hung council, or a majority of individual councillors in a less politicised situation, it is likely to be ineffective even in situations where there is formal political endorsement of the plan. It follows also that one would normally expect a link between party manifestos of majority or co-operating parties and corporate strategy. Political manifestos and corporate strategies are different kinds of document – but there must be a process of translation and development from the one to the other if strategy is to prove effective (see below). Indeed, one of the best ways of assessing the likely effectiveness of a corporate strategy (of which the authority of origin is not known) is to see whether it is possible to make an informed guess as to which party or parties controls the authority.

It would be expected that both the content and tone of corporate strategies would vary between the three major parties. Perceptions of role and purpose would be expected to differ, with, for example, commitments to a commercialist approach (e.g. Brent plc) being most likely in Conservative-controlled authorities. Redistribution and anti-poverty themes would be most likely in Labour-controlled authorities, and commitment to the devolution of power to local communities most likely in Liberal Democrat controlled authorities. If such areas of choice, where there are real differences of political view (or emphasis) between the major parties, are not highlighted, it becomes correspondingly likely that the strategy is operating on a symbolic set of pious generalities.

The key role of the leader in strategy

If the chief executive is the major potential champion of strategic initiatives on the officer side, it is equally true that the council leader or leader of the majority party is the major potential strategic champion on the member side. This is because just as 'corporate strategy' serves a chief executive's interests (both as a reflection of the significance of the role and as a potential source of influence on the management of the authority), so the position and influence of leader is strengthened and enhanced by his or her association with a corporate strategy. Opposition members' key role is to oppose, challenge and scrutinise effectively the operations of the majority group; that of majority party backbenchers is typically that of 'constituency advocate'; and committee chairs typically develop an over-riding commitment to the protection and enhancement of 'their' service. Leaders have no such underpinning functions for their role. As chairs of policy and resources, they are inevitably drawn into the realm of strategic corporate issues, although that does not necessarily co-exist with a predisposition to tackle such issues strategically.

Writers who have examined the role sets of political leaders have invariably concluded that 'strategic policy direction' is a dominant leadership role. One of the authors, drawing on the work of Kotter and Lawrence (1974) has identified four key political leadership roles in British local government:

1. the maintenance of group cohesiveness;

2. the initiation of strategic policy direction;

3. the representation of the authority in the external world;

4. 'making things happen' i.e. ensuring the organisation is delivering political priorities.

It is not, however, always the formal leader who becomes the most prominent 'strategic champion'. It is a role equally attractive to leadership aspirants, or to younger ambitious politicians who see strategy as a way of challenging the traditional power of the older service committee chairs. It follows that although the leader/chief executive relationship is the most likely strategic driving force (and is at the very least a necessary source of support), other combinations are possible as sources of strategic initiative: leader/head of the policy unit; deputy leader/chief executive; or rising star/head of corporate services.

Because of the intrinsic importance of identifying and responding to strategic issues to the welfare of the authority, a leader who is able to individually dominate (in conjunction with the chief executive) the way in which the strategic agenda is responded to is a more powerful leader than one who chooses or is obliged to share such responsibility. This is one of the ways in which there is still a significant difference between Conservative and Labour leaders: the former can and do still exercise more individual power in responding to a strategic agenda than the latter. That does not necessarily make them better leaders, for the real challenge of leadership in relation to strategic direction is to lead in a way which enables the authority as a whole to respond effectively to strategic issues in a manner which is compatible with the prevailing culture of the party group.

The leader/chief executive relationship

Notwithstanding what we have written earlier about the way in which the key strategic champions in a local authority may not be the leader or chief executive, the most common situation is for this partnership to constitute the main driving force for strategy, and at the very least their support is a crucial ingredient of success. Differences of view about the viability of a strategic initiative are a likely source of tension in the relationship. It is hence worthwhile exploring the dynamics of this relationship in more detail here, as it is so central to the success of strategic planning and management.

Although there are usually differences between leader and chief executive over the interpretation of the four key leadership tasks, (see p.57 above) and the relative priority attached to them, in most authorities there is a mutual recognition that each needs the other for the achievement of their separate agendas. In particular, the leader needs the chief executive to deliver, through the council's officer structure, the political priorities of the majority group (or 'coalition', or 'administration') for even if a majority group chooses to involve itself in implementation processes ('making things happen') there are clearly limits to what it can achieve directly in relation to this task. The chief executive, in particular, needs the leader to provide or agree to some kind of strategic/policy direction to provide consistent guidance to the work of officers.

The problems of a weak leadership figure in either category soon becomes obvious in authorities where this is the reality. Authorities which have experimented with dispensing with a chief executive soon become vulnerable to fragmentation on the officer side, with potential alliances between chief officers and committee chairs making the political leader's task achievement more difficult especially in relation to strategic direction and political cohesiveness. Hung authorities without chief executives often exhibit 'extreme' symptoms of fragmentation and lack of direction. In authorities which lack political leaders – either because the level of politicisation is such that the need for leadership has not been recognised or because the party groups and leaders in a hung authority can find no basis for co-operation – the onus falls on the chief officers and in particular the chief executive to fill the gap in relation to strategic direction, external representation, and sometimes political cohesiveness. However, their efforts in relation to strategic direction may often fail to generate the requisite degree of political support in either situation. Chief executives who are 'weak', either due to a lack of personal skills and influence or by political design, cannot or do not provide the necessary officer input which can help transform political priorities into realistic programmes of action. They can also leave an 'implementation' vacuum which leaders or other councillors move in to fill, at considerable cost to their other tasks and time demands. Weak leaders fail to provide the political steer and consistency of direction which chief executives need for 'task accomplishment' and increase the risk of organisational fragmentation on a service-by-service basis.

At best, the synergy between the two roles can become a driving force within the authority. The sense of a driving force can be particularly strong in relatively small shire districts, where the combination of a powerful leader with a strategic vision and a chief executive who shares it is a formidable combination indeed. In shire districts, which have a relatively limited range of responsibilities compared with other types of authority, it is possible for both leader and chief executive to have an overall grasp of the authority's business. This capacity is much more difficult to develop in a shire county or metropolitan district, where the demands on leaders and chief executives in this respect are much greater as they encompass education, social services and structure planning in addition to a range of other services. This does not mean, of course, that the effectiveness of the relationship is any less crucial to the welfare of the authority.

There is an implicit series of bargains which underpin the relationship. The first is *informational*: both the chief executive and leader can, in normal circumstances, provide an exclusive and privileged source of information for the other. The second implicit element of the bargain is *joint* (though not necessarily equal) *participation* in strategic direction in both proactive and reactive senses. Chief executives will invariably concede the right of majority party or 'administration' to play the lead role in these processes. What they require is that they and other chief officers should have the opportunity to influence the process so that the political choices made are fully informed choices. Hence the potential benefits of the informal member-officer discussion forums at whatever level they operate. Leaders can benefit in this respect from the edge which the discussions with the briefings from chief executives give them, in the task of persuading the leadership group and party group of the case for a particular course of actions. The ability to come up with workable, politically acceptable proposals to deal with problems can only strengthen the leader's reputation and authority within the group.

If there is a mutual sense that this set of implicit bargains is working fairly and effectively in overall terms, then the problems of the leader or chief executive in relation to one or other of the tasks will be understood and accepted: problems experienced by a leader, for example, in controlling or predicting the views of an unstable or factionalised group; or problems experienced by a chief executive in retaining the commitment of a maverick chief officer to a strategic direction. Both leaders and chief executives know that they have much to gain from sustaining the relationship, and that they would be in an extremely vulnerable position if it broke down.

Widening member involvement in strategy

For a strategic launch, it may be that 'political acquiescence' will suffice. However, once a strategic agenda or plan begins to raise politically contentious issues about budgetary allocations, or a public commitment to certain priorities, something more is required. Typically, strategic initiatives are launched because the chief executive and council leader decide that it is a good idea. However, there may be stronger commitment on the part of one of these parties than the other but at the very least there must be enough positive support from the leader to gain agreement within the majority group (or co-operating groups) in a balanced authority. When the strategy process begins to identify real and difficult choices, then a more proactive level of political support becomes necessary. Strategic initiatives need their political champions amongst the body of elected members, just as they do amongst middle managers.

Finding the right forums

This process of widening the political constituency of support for a strategic initiative can be helped by a persuasive leader working formally and informally with a group, sub-groups, and individuals. But an equally important potential influence is the *design* of the political machinery for taking the strategy forward. If political commitment and ownership is to be agreed, a number of conditions are important.

1. The developing strategy must be seen (at least in part) as a reflection of the de facto political direction/priorities of the majority groups/or co-operating in a balanced authority.

2. The forums in which strategic priorities are first identified and then in which programmes of action are developed to address them should be

informal in nature, with a climate very different from that of a committee or sub-committee.

3. The forums should be structured in such a way that member leadership is apparent, but member and officer roles are compatible with the nature of this task.

Each of these conditions will be examined in turn. Firstly, the link with political direction is considered. As we have already emphasised strategies are – or should be – highly political documents, reflective of political priorities. Thus, if there exists a serious political manifesto which has been used by the majority party at a recent election it will be vital to ensure that its context was taken seriously in the formulation of strategy. In the mid-1980s, a few instances were reported of authorities in which the manifesto of the newly elected majority party was adopted as 'council policy' at the first council meeting after the election, thus achieving the status of a 'de facto' strategy. Putting to one side the possible importance symbolically for the party concerned with such action, it does not represent a particularly helpful interpretation of the relationship between manifesto and strategy. Manifestos are rarely in a form which is appropriate for a corporate strategy; they typically contain a mixture of objectives which encompass the very general and the quite specific. But it is appropriate (unless the manifesto is viewed simply as a device to aid election performances) to use it as a basis for the development of a corporate strategy. It should provide an important input to the strategic agenda. Typically this process will require the majority party (or co-operating parties in a hung authority) to:

■ identify priorities amongst a long list of possible strategic issues contained in the manifesto;

■ explore the inter-relationships between these priorities – how action taken in pursuit of one objective might complement, or conflict with another;

■ identify some key choices in relation to each strategic issue, which will influence the development of possible programmes of action without, at this stage, specifying such programmes.

Thus, to stimulate the requisite degree of member commitment in the early stages of a strategic initiative, it is important to emphasise the links with the manifesto. Certainly any strategy which virtually ignores a recent manifesto is drastically reducing its prospects of political acceptability.

Secondly, what kind of forums are most appropriate for the development of strategy? The point to stress here is the importance of informality. Strategic development cannot effectively be carried out in the familiar traditional committee settings of a local authority. It requires the normal public roles of members and officers to be modified. It requires the scope for identification of possible courses of action which may subsequently be excluded as too politically contentious, too costly, or illegal. It requires brainstorming, and ad hoc officer responses to members' suggestions (and vice versa), which would be impossible in a committee setting.

Strategic development cannot effectively be carried out in the familiar traditional committee setting.

A one party or all-party approach?

One of the first judgements which has to be made in relation to a strategic launch is whether the majority party only should be involved in the informal strategy development arenas, or whether all parties should be involved. In a hung or balanced authority there is little choice but to involve all parties (although it is always possible that a self-styled 'opposition' party will decline to participate) unless there is a de facto coalition between two or more parties who may then choose to exclude parties not involved in the coalition from the strategy formulation process. Clearly, all strategies that are formally tabled at committee or council then become subject to all-party debate. Where there is a choice, much depends upon the political culture of the authority and in particular the relationships between the respective party groups. In a highly politicised authority, with a tradition of inter-group conflict, it is highly unlikely that a majority group would wish to involve a minority group in the strategy formulation process. After all, if a strategy is an intrinsically political document, with a clear link to the party manifesto, then it is difficult to see what value there would be in informal discussions between, for example, a right-wing 'minimalist' Conservative group and a radical Labour group. There is, of course, political capital to be made from such 'informal' discussions. Bright ideas, which may not subsequently prove practicable or politically acceptable when scrutinised more carefully may well emerge in such occasions and indeed such ideas should be encouraged. Any indication that an opposition member might 'leak' such ideas to the press would quickly end any attempt at inter-party co-operation in strategy formulation.

On the other hand in authorities which are still relatively un-politicised in party terms (e.g. where group discipline is embryonic), where inter-party relations are good, or where the opposition is at such a token level numerically that there is little political point in exclusion, it is much less likely that gains in political capital will be sought and the case for all-party involvement, at least in the early stages of the process, is much stronger. The main potential benefit is that a strategy with all-party support provides increased legitimacy in discussion or negotiation with outside interests, or in bids for external funding (particularly if the local 'opposition' is from the same party as the national government of the day). The potential danger is that in the process of attempting to reach inter-party consensus, the strategy is de-politicised and moves into the realms of increasingly meaningless generalities.

One possibility is to set out a corporate strategy in two parts, one of which has all-party support, and the other the support of the majority party only. Despite the case for the link with party manifestos, many of the strategic issues set out in recent examples received by the authors do not appear a likely source of party division in themselves. Dealing with crime, preventative health, city centre regeneration, environmental sustainability are all strategic issues which have the possibility at least of inspiring all-party support, although when the process moves on to the means of tackling the issues it is perhaps more likely that party-related difference of view will emerge. The search for consensus is certainly worthwhile, so long as it does not result in a blurring of choice and dilution of strategic content.

Design criteria for strategic arenas

The design challenge, therefore, is to identify a type of informal forum with which members feel at ease. This task is not as straightforward as it perhaps sounds. There are a number of potential pitfalls. The size of the forum has to be appropriate: it is hard to sustain the right kind of atmosphere for an informal discussion if more than a dozen people are present. In addition, if numbers do rise above this level it becomes increasingly likely that discussion will be dominated by a small proportion of the participants. It may be symbolically important that members outnumber, or at least are not outnumbered by, officers. Certainly the forum should be member-chaired, and it should be clear in both procedural and cultural terms that it is being member-led. The advisory role of officers should be made clear, although there are considerable advantages if officers are able to participate as equals (under Chatham House rules). The setting may be important too. If it is possible to escape from the traditional climate and associations of the committee room so much the better.

One authority which has invested a good deal of organisational time and energy into trying to identify and develop an appropriate type of forum for member involvement in strategic formulation is Barnsley MDC. Over a period of 5 years since 1991, the authority has established 20 strategic review workshops or topics defined by members themselves, covering corporate priorities (e.g. anti-poverty), service areas (e.g. education), and management issues (e.g. asset management). These workshops have been introduced with the following aims:

The Barnsley MDC approach

- To provide greater clarity of the objectives and priorities of the Council as a whole, leading to greater shared understanding between sectional interests.

- To ensure elected members have ownership of policy/strategy and priorities across all services.

- To support the proper management of services, within agreed policy/strategy.

- To provide for systems of review, leading both to better management performance, and refinement or change of policy/strategy where/when necessary.

The expectation was that the workshops would operate in the following way:

- small (6–9 elected members and officer support);

- member led, with free and frank discussion between members and officers;

- in sub-committees members ask questions and officers answer. In workshops officers ask questions: 'what are you trying to achieve?', 'what do you want this service to deliver?';

- all-party;

- to recommend to Council on broad policy/strategy;

- not constrained by finance, but recommended policy/strategy subject to finance availability;

- limited time-span. Workshops are intended to complete their task over 6–12 months (depending on its complexity), to make a report to group and then to operate (if appropriate) only on 'care and maintenance' basis.

At a recent seminar attended by one of the authors, the effectiveness of this mechanism was reviewed, and although various detailed proposals for change were made, the general view was that the strategic review workshops were effective as a way of involving significant numbers of members in strategy formulation.

The politics of strategy in hung authorities

The uncertainties of the balanced situation make strategic planning particularly difficult. The need to continuously build majorities for particular decisions, and the delicate negotiations that are necessary both within party groups and between them, in order to build these majorities, encourages parties to adopt a short-term perspective, rather than a longer-term, more strategic vision. This is despite the fact that the need for strategic planning is probably greater in a balanced authority where the consistency and stability of practical agreements are likely to be less certain. A number of authorities have been able to point to strategic plans that have developed while the council was balanced, and which have been largely successful. Evidence of short-termism is not supported by an investigation which Leicestershire county council (1987) held into procedures for 'financial and policy planning, resource allocation and policy/performance review' in hung counties. Their report found that:

> *In five counties planning and review processes that operated before the loss of overall control had continued to operate since, and that although some changes and adjustments had been necessary, in no case had there been a significant reduction in the effectiveness of the processes.*

Even more significantly, in the remaining 13 hung county councils examined, all had actually considerably developed their planning and review processes since becoming hung. While it was undeniable that in some of these authorities long-term planning had become more difficult:

> *It is a surprising but important finding that the loss of overall control has in the shire counties either allowed the survival or development of such processes, or in some cases has actually encouraged them.*

It is important to note that in the learning processes involved in managing a hung council, the problems identified are capable of resolution:

> *It does not necessarily follow, therefore, the hung authorities will lead to inconsistencies in policies; the fact that the problems are more obvious in a hung authority may actually*

stimulate a focus on strengthening policy-making, based on the identification of areas of party agreement.

If an authority is unstable and unable to reach agreement on ways of working then policy-making will be difficult and forward planning less likely. But the majority do not fit this description, and even those that do tend to experience difficulty only at certain times.

There are important differences in emphasis in approach to strategic planning in hung authorities. First, officers, and especially the chief executive, have a major role to play in influencing and developing strategic thinking in balanced authorities. This is a role which many chief executives have been happy to pursue. One of the most common approaches adopted by chief executives who want their balanced authority to adopt a more strategic approach to issues has been to prepare a working paper on the problems or challenges facing the council. Where used, this approach has been largely successful in encouraging the different party groups to debate their strategic visions in response to the issues raised, and to adopt particular strategic plans. For example, Warwickshire County Council went through this type of process in 1988, leading to a strategic plan that has formed the basis for its policies over the last seven years, despite the fact that control of the Council has switched from a minority Labour leadership to majority Conservative control (between 1989 and 1993) and back to a minority Labour leadership. The outcome, however, has been a concentration on managerial reform of the council, rather than more ideologically driven change. Thus, the strategy has concentrated upon such issues as the management of the council's computing resources and the development of 'customer care plans'. More ideologically motivated strategies have been noticeably absent.

Indeed, groups who wish to pursue ideologically inspired strategies will be most successful if they can dress up their proposals in more managerial terms, and gain general support for their initiatives from officers. Consequently, rather than attempting to gain support from other parties for particular initiatives, groups pursuing strategic plans will be most successful if they can communicate their proposals as managerial reforms which do not relate directly to any ideological agenda.

Conclusion

It is clear from what has been written in Chapters 5 and 6 that an understanding of the political and organisational context of the development of strategic initiatives is crucial in a number of different ways.

- It demonstrates that the introduction of an explicit strategic dimension into the operations of a local authority – or the continuation, revival or re-direction of an existing initiative – are processes which are likely to be contested within a local authority. There are a number of political concerns (flexibility and short-termism, particularly in the run up to local elections; avoidance of over-explicit goals which may prove unattainable) and organisational concerns (protection of departmental autonomy and budget flows) which may be threatened by the introduction or extension of a strategic initiative. In these circumstances explicit or tacit resistance would normally be expected.

- It provides pointers to the appropriateness of different strategic approaches. An astute reading of an authority's tradition and culture will provide a guide as to what is possible (in the short term) and what is impossible.

- By the same token it provides evidence of the kind of cultural changes which are needed to strengthen the strategic dimension in the longer term.

- It demonstrates the need for strategic champions and allies around which the strategic initiative can be organised.

- It will often reveal one or more opportunities which can be exploited to give the strategic initiative momentum (e.g. the retirement of a treasurer who has hitherto opposed the initiative; an opportunity to bid for external resources where a strategic context has to be demonstrated; growing opposition to a 'fair shares' approach to budgetary cuts).

The need for champions and allies overlaps the member/officer interface. Committed chief executives need allies and champions within the ruling group (or coalition) as well as within the officer establishment. Enthusiastic leaders need them amongst officers, as well, or within their own party group. Sometimes it is possible to identify a point in the development of a strategic initiative where a critical mass of support in an appropriate range of places is reached which enables the initiative to 'take off' or move up the agenda. In hung authorities, as we have seen, this process is a particularly difficult and delicate one, in which the range of possible influence opportunities within and between the member and officer worlds increases, but the task of building a majority coalition is a particularly daunting one. A more detailed assessment of the ways in which coalition of support may be built up is provided in Chapter 10.

Many recent publications which have addressed the implication for elected members of the changing roles of local authorities – in particular of the change of emphasis from 'providing' to 'enabling' – have concluded that the strategic role of councillors is one which ought to be highlighted and strengthened (see Audit Commission 1996; DoE 1993; Labour Party 1995). This conclusion is certainly supported and echoed by our analysis of the enhanced importance of corporate strategies (*see* Chapter 2) and the need for councillors to play a leading role in their formulation, if such strategies are to prove effective (see pp.48–50 above). In our view, however, it is important to be realistic about the extent to which strategic planning is likely to appeal to local councillors. In most of the authorities in which we have worked, it would be regarded as luxury if as many as a dozen councillors were genuinely interested in issues of corporate strategy. Many will be much more concerned with specific services or with the needs of their local constituents. The challenge in a strategic initiative is to gain the acceptance of the majority of councillors who have other priorities and to show that it is a worthwhile activity, and then to try to find ways in which as many as possible can become actively involved in strategic planning or review processes. It should be recognised, however, that the process is likely in most authorities to generate positive interest and enthusiasm amongst a minority of councillors only.

SUMMARY

- Strategic planning and management are by their nature 'political' processes in that:

  (i) they imply a re-allocation of resources between different sub-divisions of the local authority (department, committees etc);

  (ii) they have a basis in party political priorities, and the development of such priorities into actions.

- In any discussion about strategic planning, there would be an expectation that politicians would wish to be less specific about intentions and leave greater scope for short-term manoeuvring than would officers.

- Any strategic plan or planning process which does not connect with and in some sense reflect the priorities and ways of working of majority parties (or co-operating parties in a hung council) is likely to prove ineffective.

- The chief executive is the most important potential 'strategic champion' amongst the officers and the council leader the most important political champion amongst the members.

- The initiation of strategic direction has been identified as one of the four key political leadership roles, the others being:

(i)   the maintenance of groups cohesiveness;

(ii) the representation of the authority in the outside world;

(iii) ensuring the organisation has the capacity to deliver political priorities.

- At best the synergy between the two roles of chief executive and council leader can become the key driving force for corporate strategy within the authority.

- The uncertainties associated with the hung and balanced council make strategic planning more difficult, despite the intensified need for strategic planning in such authorities. With politically sensitive management, however, the introduction or consolidation of such initiative is possible.

- In hung authorities, groups advocating corporate strategies will be most successful if they can present their proposals as management reforms which do not relate directly to any ideological agenda.

- When the strategy process begins to identify real and difficult choices, then a more proactive level of political support becomes necessary. Strategic initiatives need their political champions amongst the body of elected members, just as they do amongst middle managers.

- This process of widening the political constituency of support for a strategic initiative can be helped by a persuasive leader working formally and informally with a group, sub-groups, and individuals. But an equally important potential influence is the design of the political machinery for taking the strategy forward.

  (i)   The forums in which strategic priorities are first identified and then in which programmes of action are developed to address them should be informal in nature, with a climate very different from that of a committee or sub-committee.

  (ii) The forums should be structured in such a way that member leadership is apparent, but member and officer roles are compatible with the nature of this task.

  (iii) In a highly politicised authority, with a tradition of inter-group conflict, it is highly unlikely that a majority group would wish to involve a minority group in the strategy formulation process (or indeed that a minority party would wish to be so involved).

  (iv) In authorities which are still relatively un-politicised in party terms or where inter-party relations are good (or where the opposition is at such a token level numerically that there is a little political point in exclusion), the case for all-party involvement is strong.

- Strategic forums are most effective when their membership is relatively small and their operation is time-limited.

7

Core values and mission statements

INTRODUCTION

There is a seductive charm about core values and mission statements. They are relatively easy to write and full of positive messages. Terms like 'customer-friendly', 'businesslike' and 'partnership' roll off the tongue. However, they are often extremely difficult to put into practice, in a way which reflects real cultural change. Indeed there are three key questions which should be asked about any core value.

- What does it mean?

- Is there an alternative core value which implies doing things differently?

- What difference will it make to the culture and behaviour of the organisation?

The importance of core values was highlighted in a number of influential private management texts of the 1980s for example the famous *In Search of Excellence*. In it Peters and Waterman (1982, p.279) describe the significance of 'core values' thus:

> Let us suppose that we were asked for one all-purpose bit of advice for management, one truth that we were able to distil from the 'excellent companies' research. We might be tempted to reply 'figure out your value system: decide what your company stands for . . . clarifying the value system and breathing life into it are the greatest contributions a leader can make.

Little attention had previously been paid to core values in local government management agendas in Britain. But local authorities – particularly those with ambitious chief executives – soon picked up the language. Local authority job advertisements began to appear under symbols which announced what the authority's dominant core value were:

> Braintree means Business
>
> Wolverhampton: The Pace Setter
>
> Harrow: A Sensible London Borough
>
> Working for Quality and Equality (Ealing)
>
> Caring and Winning Through (Basildon)
>
> Where People Come First (Southwark)

It is easy to be cynical or sceptical about such epithets, and they have now largely disappeared from sight. But they were interesting as pioneering attempts to say something specific about the dominant cultural characteristics of the authority concerned: don't expect anything too radical or experimental in Harrow but watch Wolverhampton for new innovations; Basildon saw local government (in the 1980s) as some kind of battle while nearby Braintree clearly saw itself as running a business.

Core values

What we have seen in the 1990s is a proliferation of statements of core values. From analysis of our survey material it is possible to distinguish the following most popular themes:

- business-like
- competitive
- value for money
- partnership
- citizenship
- community
- customer-orientation

- service quality

- communication

- consultation

- equality

- accessibility

- valuing staff

- civic pride

- caring.

Here are some examples, taken at random, which illustrate the kind of statements which local authorities are currently making in relation to these themes.

Partnership

The council will seek to act in partnership with its residents, customers, schools, contractors, the business community, the voluntary sector, the health services, the police, other local agencies and with the Central Government . . . it will pursue its aim through genuine consultation and by actively using all channels of influence by providing Civic and Community Leadership.

(London Borough of Redbridge)

Valuing the workforce

The council's most important resource is its workforce. It will seek to deal fairly with all employees, offering them the necessary training and resources to do their job properly as well as creating a working environment that encourages personal responsibility, mutual respect and innovation, and, wherever possible, the chance to progress within the organisation.

(Calderdale MBC)

Customer care

The council will be responsive and courteous to individuals and groups. The people served by the council will be treated fairly and honestly. Comments or complaints from the public will be considered carefully and responded to both directly and in future service development. The needs of our customers will be major factors in all that the council does.

(Tameside MBC)

Accountability and choice

People have limited choice in the services they receive from the council. As a public monopoly in so many respects our duty is to ensure that the balance of power is shifted from those who control and deliver services to those who use them. This will be achieved by making service provision accountable to people in their neighbourhood.

(Walsall MBC)

Public service

The belief that there is much that is valuable and estimable about an organisation which is devoted to the greater good of the community as a whole and of the individuals within it, and is not merely founded on the unbridled pursuit of private material advantage.

(City of Bristol)

Community

To empower communities and encourage local leadership from within them through consultation, information provision and increased participation in decision making.

(Shropshire CC)

Equality

We want to give a fairer deal to those suffering discrimination, and to disadvantaged and vulnerable groups. We will take positive action to improve our services and our own employment practices for those who are poor, to women, minority ethnic groups, the elderly, people with disabilities, and to lesbians and gay men. We will support efforts by these groups to develop self-help services.

(Brighton Borough Council)

Communication

We recognise the importance of making both the people we serve, and our own employees, aware of what we are doing and why. We also acknowledge that good communication is a two-way process and that we must listen to what is said to us.

(Great Yarmouth Borough Council)

This selection of core value statements well illustrates some of the similarities, differences and overlaps of the genre. The style and generality of language (and, in most cases, the incontestability) are similar. However, there are differences in form. The City of Bristol's view of 'public service' is a clear statement of ideological belief with no action implications drawn out. On the other hand, Calderdale's statement on 'valuing the workforce' and Brighton's statement on 'equality', both go into some detail about how they will endeavour to put the value into practice (note, for example, the self-help element in the latter). There is a good deal of overlap apparent in the examples. Walsall's statement on accountability and choice is also as much about empowerment and community; Shropshire's statement on community also mentions communication and participation. The important point to stress is that in the form set out, all the examples of core values included have the potential to change organisational behaviour – but equally the capacity to operate only as PR symbols.

There is certainly growing evidence of a highly sceptical view of core values and mission statements epitomised by Midwinter and McGarvey (1995). They have written in the light of their survey of the development of such practices in Scotland.

Overall, we would question the ability of mission statements and the like as management tools ... It may be that such statements have more to do with public relations than the internal management of local authorities.

Their view of mission statements in particular is singularly dismissive:

What struck us about these documents was their neutrality: all the missions or values would be perfectly acceptable to almost everyone, and it is difficult to see what guidance they give council managers in the day to day implementation of their tasks. These typically consist of bland statements of how much a council values its employees, service performance and care for its customers ... over ten local authorities (in Scotland) strove to improve the quality of life of their citizens! We suspect it could be difficult to find an authority which did not have this admirable objective.

Such cynicism is, to some extent at least, justified by a provisional content analysis of the documentation received in connection with the our survey (and by some examples already provided). However it would be premature to dismiss mission statements per se as tokenism or public relations. There are authorities for whom mission statements have made a significant impact on organisational culture, or have been seen as a necessary stage in changing culture, by making clear the philosophy.

At their most superficial, local authority 'core values' statements merit the general criticism meted out by Midwinter and McGarvey. Quality, in particular, is an elusive concept, and to give real substance to it as a value is beyond the ability of many authorities. What, for example, is the following (anonymous) example really saying?

> **Quality, in particular, is an elusive concept, and to give real substance to it as a value is beyond many authorities.**

The Council strives to provide the widest range and highest quality of services to its customers, in line with agreed priorities and standards, limited only by available resources.

It would be hard to find a council that wasn't!

The reality – or unreality – of value choices

The first real test of a core value lies in the extent to which it expresses an identifiable choice. For example, the choices expressed in the 'Fitness for Purpose' dimensions and illustrative examples imply different views of what an authority sees as its primary role. One would, therefore, expect different choices made at this level to have implications for the core values subsequently identified as important. Commercialist local authorities are likely to emphasise values such as 'businesslike', 'competition', and 'value for money'. Authorities committed to the community governance role are more likely to emphasise 'partnership' and 'citizenship'. Those committed to a neighbourhood approach are likely to highlight 'community' and 'participation', traditional direct service providers, the benefits of 'public service' and 'service quality'. The display below provides a categorisation of core values by dominant role.

'Fitness for purpose': dimensions and core values

Belief in Market values	c.f. Belief in Public Service values
■ Choice	■ Responsiveness to need
■ Competition	■ Public service ethos
■ Businesslike	■ Co-operation
Emphasis on Wider Governmental Role	c.f. Emphasis on Service Provision Role
■ Partnership	■ Value for money
■ Entrepreneurship and opportunity taking	■ Customer orientation
Emphasis on Individualism	Emphasis on Communities
■ Choice	■ Citizenship
■ Consumerism	■ Community orientation
■ Consultation	■ Participation

Similarly, irrespective of whether or not a local authority explicitly makes this kind of fundamental value choice, we would argue that there is a real choice – of emphasis at the very least – between certain pairs of core values. For example:

■ choice between competition . . . and co-operation;

■ choice between customer (or consumer) orientation . . . and citizenship;

- choice between customers . . . and communities;

- choice between communication . . . and participation.

There is, for example, a world of difference between an entrepreneurial culture in which business units are expected to compete with each other and with external agencies and a co-operative culture in which staff are encouraged to work together to resolve problems facing the authority. An emphasis on citizenship implies civic duties and responsibilities (as well as rights) on the part of the authority's residents whereas the values of customer-orientation and consumerism emphasise only rights to equal service and choice. Authorities which are highly sceptical about participative democracy may well be prepared to emphasise the importance of good communication and consultation with residents, while authorities with a belief in 'participative democracy' are likely to highlight participation itself as a value. Other core values require further elaboration if they are to convey a sense of real choice:

- partnership – with whom and to what end?

- community-oriented – in what sense? City-wide? Local or interest group based?

- equality – of what? Access? Provision? In relation to need?

As noted earlier a good test of the significance of a core value is whether an alternative can be identified that would imply a different mode of behaviour or a different conception of role and purpose. If this is not possible, then the value becomes vulnerable to the Midwinter and McGarvey charge of 'would anyone be likely to disagree with it?'. 'Quality service' runs that risk, unless an authority can provide a particular interpretation of quality which moves it beyond its current 'buzz-word' status. Similar problems are inherent in phrases like 'value for money' and 'positive staff evaluation'.

In summary, if a core value can be related to real choices about an authority's role and purpose it becomes possible to apply the 'alternative' test – 'we are clear we want to be a co-operative not a competitive authority'. In some cases, the choice is not an either/or one, but rather whether an authority wants to move beyond a particular value. Most authorities are likely to be concerned about customers; the key question is whether that is the limit of their relationship with the local population, or whether 'community' and/or 'citizenship' are seen as additional values.

The testing of core values

One of the most helpful ways of illustrating the dilemmas of developing a statement of core values which moves beyond the level of 'of course' statements and actually influences (or has the potential to influence) they way the authority actually operates, is to examine some examples, and to subject them to the kind of tests already identified.

- Is the meaning of the value clear?

- Is there an 'alternative' value which could plausibly be adopted?

- Have middle-managers and staff working directly with the public internalised the values?

- Is it clear how the authority will know if it has effectively operationalised the values?

The first example shown below is taken from the London Borough of Sutton, a pioneer in the use of core values and strategic priorities, which produced in

---

Sutton Council aims to build a community in which all can take part and all can take pride. We are committed to:

- Working in PARTNERSHIP with the people who live or work in the Borough.

- Enabling and encouraging INVOLVEMENT at the Council's decision-making processes.

- Making our services open and ACCESSIBLE so that everyone should feel able to approach us with confidence, be listened to and treated with respect.

- Providing HIGH QUALITY, COST EFFECTIVE SERVICES which meet community needs in a changing environment.

- Promoting EQUALITY where everyone is treated fairly but taking account of the special needs in a changing environment.

- INVESTING WISELY FOR THE FUTURE, protecting and developing human and natural resources to ensure a healthy environment for present and future generations.

- The Council also recognises that its MOST IMPORTANT ASSET IS ITS STAFF, who have a key role in promoting price in our community through the adoption of these core values.

1992 the following statement of core values – a set of fundamental beliefs underpinning the way in which all activities are to be carried out.

Some of the core values set out in the list are refreshingly different. 'Investing Wisely for the Future' expresses a clear commitment to long-term environmental sustainability in the Borough. The theme of 'accessibility' though less original is developed in such a way that progress towards it is measurable. 'Equality' is given 'special needs' interpretation which distinguishes it from other authorities' views. 'Involvement' signals a construct to participatory democracy which goes beyond the more prevalent values of 'communication' and 'consultation'. The other values are perhaps more predictable. But the statement overall passes the key test of saying something about Sutton which distinguishes it from other differently inclined authorities.

A less convincing statement of core values is provided by an authority which shall be nameless.

Why we're here – our core values

- We view the public as our customers, and we must improve the quality of our services to them, ensuring that our services continue to adapt to meet changing needs.

- We are committed to improving the cost effectiveness of our services.

- We believe that effective and efficient spending on local services is vital to the well being of local people and the health of the Borough's economy.

- We are striving to be a good equal opportunities employer, and to ensure that all sections of the community, especially the disadvantaged, have access to our services.

- We will improve communications with the public – listening harder and producing better information.

- We recognise that managers, workers and customers, as well as politicians have ideas for improving services.

- We will strive to make the Borough a better place to live and work.

- We will take a lead in promoting a pride in the Borough.

It is not that these values are not laudable – far from it! However, apart from a concern with disadvantaged, with its overtures of 'positive discrimination', there is little in the statement with which any authority would be likely to disagree. The list would be equally applicable to most other authorities and hence says little or nothing about what is distinctive about this particular borough council.

John Stewart (1995b) develops the point about 'testability' in his recent paper in which he raises the questions of what differences core values make, and how anyone would know:

> Many local authorities have produced statements of organisational values. There remains uncertainty how far these statements are embedded in the organisation. There is an ever-present danger that actions by the authority, far from reinforcing the values, are perceived as changing them. A statement about a valued staff, followed after a short interval by redundancy notices may not be a rejection of the value, but will certainly be seen as such.

Stewart goes on to argue that:

> One of the problems about statements of organisational values is that they are often left hanging in the air. It is not clear what they mean in practice or even what they could or should mean in practice. The issue is how is an authority that supports these values is supposed to differ from one that does not do so – not merely in the day-to-day working, but in dealing with difficult issues.

There is a need to develop techniques for testing the values in:

- preparing the statement;
- explaining the statement.

This could be done by a series of mini-cases or examples.

- If we really believe in this value it will mean that we would behave in this way.
- If we believe in this statement it will mean that we would not behave in this way.

It is only through a testing series of core values in this way that it can be established:

- that they are really believed in;
- that they are understood.

One of the authors was involved in an LGMB-commissioned study of the 16 local authorities which (in 1992) were perceived by a large sample of chief executives as being the best managed in England. Several of the authorities possessed core value (or mission) statements which were typically highlighted by the chief executive as a contribution to 'good management'. An opportunity for discovering the extent to which the values had spread beyond the management team was provided by a meeting, in each authority, with a group of middle managers. In some cases the managers concerned were not even aware of the existence of the mission statement; in others they knew of its existence and were familiar (more or less) with its contents, but did not consider that they really affected the way they or their staff operated. In a small number, however, there was evidence of both knowledge and application. The values had been to some extent at least internalised and operationalised. That experience demonstrates both the ultimate challenge and the pitfalls of mission statements. They can, in the right circumstances transform the operating culture of the authority; but they can also serve a predominantly symbolic function – proudly displayed to visiting researchers but unrecognised once one gets beyond the authority's management team! If the test of a strategic vision lies in its influence on the budget (*see* Chapter 8), the test of a mission statement lies in its influence on the way things are done in the authority.

> **Mission statements can transform the operating culture of the authority; but they can also serve a predominantly symbolic function.**

It is, in principle, possible to devise tests which establish whether the adoption of a core value has made a difference. In relation to customer-responsiveness, Skelcher (1992) has identified the following criteria.

External Relationships:

- information collection: market research surveys, consultation exercises, ward meetings, user panels, 'phone-ins', opinion cards at service outlets;

- information provision: improved leaflets, translation and signing services, strengthened public relations, use of local media, open days, corporate image, public viewdata terminals, keeping employees and councillors informed;

- access: improved reception facilities, single access points for range of services, neighbourhood offices, improved telephone systems, duty managers, managers on reception desks, physical access for prams and wheelchairs, complaints hot-lines;

■ service delivery: investing in employees through training, etc., statements of customers' rights, service guarantee, developing problem-solving role of customer contact employees, redress and compensation systems, monitoring praise and complaints, removing job demarcation, investment in information technology, quality assurance systems.

Internal Operation:

■ performance indicators: systematic public opinion polling, service sampling by managers, user involvement in service redesign, monitoring members' surgeries;

■ organisational culture: service days/teams, quality circles, devolving managerial responsibility and budgets, clarifying internal and customer relationships, 'management by walking round', quality-focused policies (recruitment, induction and training), 90 day challenge, internal secondment, 'patch'/neighbourhood focused multi-disciplinary teams, total quality management.

Fluctuations in participation can be statistically demonstrated. Success in being businesslike can be measured by profitability (where this is an appropriate measure) and staff attitudes to this value by appropriate questionnaires of business units. Even 'quality' can be assessed, although not particularly conclusively, by the number of BS5570 certificates!

Conclusion

The potential benefits of mission or core value statements are by no means insubstantial.

■ They require the authority to think through what principles or beliefs they really want to adopt (amongst a large and increasing menu of choice).

■ They provide the basis of an understanding (or even a contract) between the authority and the public.

■ They provide a set of reference points for staff which can potentially integrate diverse behaviour into a more integrated whole.

■ They can enhance organisational motivation and self-esteem if they are perceived as improving organisational performance.

There are however potential pitfalls.

■ The potential gap between expectation and performance. An authority which publicly states its commitment to a set of values and then transparently fails to live up to some or all of them is in a worse position than if it had never stated them. Expectation will have increased, while performance remains unchanged.

■ Confusion, relating to unresolved conflict between values (or uncertainties as to the meaning to be attached): there are circumstances where it is impossible to be entrepreneurial and consultative (or alternatively business-like and caring) at the same time.

The implication is that the development of core values and mission statements is not a process to be undertaken lightly. As with all elements of corporate strategy it requires real political involvement and commitment if it is to become effective – not least because its success implies a significant level of resource allocation to training. The potential for superficiality and indeed ridicule is often high. But core values and mission statements represent a key element in corporate strategies – an important cultural expression and amplification of what the authority thinks it is there for. Strategic visions which are discussed in the next chapter, are the expression of an authority's external agenda for action – what problems it wishes to confront and how mission statements reflect more a desired 'internal state' for the authority; how it wishes to be seen and experienced in its day-to-day operations.

SUMMARY

It is important to:

■ ensure that the statement of core values reflects the authority's view of its role and purpose, whether this has been explicitly stated or is implicitly held;

■ ensure that core values express elected members' priorities, and that the values are fully understood by members and supported by them (on an all-party basis if possible, but certainly throughout the majority party, or coalition);

■ limit the number of core values for adoption to around half-a-dozen (or at least prioritise six or less from a large list). Otherwise the authority may appear to be trying to be 'all things to all men';

- try to define each core value in such a way that it expresses a genuine choice, i.e. so that it is possible to imagine another authority rejecting that value in favour of an alternative;

- develop a set of tests for each core value, so that its action implications (i.e. how the authority will behave and will not behave in the light of the value) are fully developed;

- involve members of staff at all levels at two stages (i) in discussions to explore the behavioural implications of each value and (ii) to ensure that each value is fully understood and internalised;

- try to devise means of assessing the extent to which the value has changed behaviour and had the desired external impact emphasising the learning mode and without becoming too rigid about quantitative assessments.

8

Strategic priorities and strategic visions

INTRODUCTION

In the previous section the case for mission statements was discussed, and the pitfalls which are associated with such initiatives identified. Although the distinction between 'mission' and 'vision' is not always clear in current local authority usage, our own view is that the two terms do have distinctive meanings, which should be reflected in the way they are used. Whereas the term 'mission' refers to the overall purpose of an organisation – what we are here for and, in particular, how that purpose is expressed in a set of core values, the term 'vision' implies an end product, a sense of what impact an authority is striving to achieve!

'Vision' implies a mental picture of what members and officers would like their area to be like in five or ten years time. Do they want a traffic-free town centre? a more diverse economy? a greener more sustainable environment? an increased sense of security in residential areas? or a revitalisation of the area's most deprived housing estate? They may of course want all of these desirable outcomes, which in itself raises two of the key challenges of strategic visions. If, as it is realistic to assume, a number of desirable outcomes are competing for scarce resources, then choices will have to be made, at least at the level of prioritisation. Is a traffic-free town centre more important than the revitalisation of a deprived housing estate, or less? Such choices become highlighted at budget-setting time. The other challenge relates to the inter-relationship between key objectives. The development of a more diverse (or a strengthened) economy may adversely affect the achievement of a greener, more sustainable environment, and vice versa. These two elements – prioritisation of objectives and the inter-relationship between them – are at the heart of the development of a strategic vision.

Mission statements – with their capacity to prove hostages to fortune – are perhaps more promising targets for criticism than strategic visions. Certainly Midwinter and McGarvey (1995) reserve their strongest criticism for the former and say relatively little about the latter. And indeed, for an authority which has expressly adopted a community governance role, the development of both a strategic vision and an agenda of strategic issues can be argued to be an essential element in carrying out this role.

The problem is that just as mission statement initiatives are strewn with pitfalls, so too are strategic vision projects. If glib allusions to 'quality' and 'partnership' leave mission statements open to ridicule, then the equivalent 'Achilles heel' of strategic visions is the listing of a series of desired end states, unquestionable in their desirability, but implausible as medium-term guides to action. 'Decent affordable housing for all' and 'adequately paid work opportunities for all who seek them' constitute 'of course' statements with which no-one is going to disagree and which are thus unlikely to affect the operation of a local authority.

The challenge of strategic planning is to find the right level at which to pitch the contents of a strategic vision. The tendency to emphasise desirable but impracticable end states is one serious limitation. But there are several others:

The challenge of strategic planning is to find the right level at which to pitch the contents of a strategic vision.

- a strategic agenda dominated by service issues, rather than issues which transcend service responsibilities;

- statements of specific projects or planned activities, the relationship of which to a broader objective is unexplained;

- too long a list of strategic issues, with priorities between the items left unclear;

- no exploration of the inter-relationship between different strategic issues.

In a strategic agenda or vision containing some or all of these limitations, there is a very real doubt about the extent to which political commitment is likely to be sustained, beyond an initial acceptance of a superficially impressive document! At their best, strategic visions provide a direction which shapes major expenditure and investment decisions. At worst, they gather dust on chief executives' shelves.

What can we learn from those authorities which have moved beyond end-state desiderata and developed strategic visions which have made a significant impact on organisational behaviour? The first key requirement is to be clear about what constitutes a corporate strategic issue. The second is the capacity to inter-relate positive and negative features of such issues.

Service issues and strategic issues

Let us consider first the extent to which service issues are legitimate items in a corporate strategy. Most of what a local authority does can be justified in terms of responding to local needs. But much of the process of doing so involves the relatively routine provision or administration of specific services. Although these activities are undeniably important to those who receive them, they do not form part of the corporate strategic agenda of the authority. This agenda concerns those issues which are of importance to the authority as a whole, and which has implications for all or some of its constituent departments. It follows that, exceptional circumstances apart, an issue which involves one specific service (department/committee) but not others is not an appropriate topic for a corporate strategic agenda. That is not to deny that it may be of strategic importance to the department concerned. However, what is a strategic issue for a department is not usually a strategic issue for the authority as a whole. There are examples of strategies which are compiled by asking each department or committee to identify its strategic priorities, followed by a process in which these priorities were compared and subjected to an authority-wide prioritisation process (usually by the policy and resources committee). The resulting document constitutes an authority-wide strategy only in a very limited sense – it provides a basis for cross-service comparison and resource allocation but does not look beyond the perceptions and programmes of service departments to a wider corporate agenda.

There are, however, situations in which a service issue involves such a fundamental change or develops such a high political profile that it does become an appropriate topic for a corporate strategy. One example is provided by the intention of a London borough in the late 1980s to abolish the grammar school element of the borough's educational system. Although strictly a service issue the political energy (and local media and pressure group attention) it generated reached such proportions that it became a 'de facto' corporate strategic issue. A more recent example is the concern felt by local authorities where the degree to which local schools are threatening to opt out of local authority control in moves to GMS (grant maintained status) has reached such proportions that the viability of the status of the authority as an effective LEA (local education authority) is threatened. 'Low educational achievement' may be a problem, as in Islington, where one of the four corporate priorities for 1996–97 is exam results.

> The Council and its secondary schools are making strenuous efforts to help local children improve their exam results. All students should reach their potential and as many as possible gain the high grades at GCSE that are so important for their future.
>
> (LB Islington)

This priority is followed by a number of measures designed to improve skills, help governors and improve attendance.

Exceptionally, therefore, service issues can legitimately be included on corporate strategic agendas but they should certainly not be dominant. Such agendas would normally be expected to focus not on service issues but on issues for which some, all or no service department currently had an interest or responsibility, or on an external change which requires major organisational change. Examples include:

1. A *territorial area* within the authority which is perceived as in some sense problematical and requiring integrated remedial action from a range of different departments and increasingly outside agencies also. Town centres may be viewed in this way, or economically declining inner city areas, or 'problem' council estates. The important criteria is that there is a perceived problem to which the council gives a high priority, and on which it wishes to concentrate attention and resources. For example:

> To develop Bexleyheath as the Borough's strategic centre by increasing the range and diversity of its shopping, office and leisure facilities, whilst also taking steps to revitalise the district shopping centre at Erith, Sidcup, Crayford and Welling.
>
> (LB Bexley)

> The continued development of Chelmsford as the premier cultural, retail, office and employment centre of Essex (The 'Emerging City' Programme).
>
> (Chelmsford BC)

2. An *age-group*, which, in the same way, the council wishes to single out for priority attention, co-ordinated action, and resources. Some councils have identified the elderly, some the under fives, other 'young people' in these terms. For example:

> The growing numbers of very elderly people have implications for a wide range of services, which will need to take into account the relative poverty of many in this group. The response to these changes must focus on older people as citizens with an interest in all aspects of the life of the town, not merely as recipients of care service.
>
> (Wolverhampton MBC)

3. A *socio-economic category*, for example, the unemployed, those living in poverty, the homeless or single parent families or an *ethnic group*, which the council wishes to single out for positive discrimination. Those local authorities which have developed equal opportunities initiatives beyond legal requirements are in effect expressing their commitment to inter (ethnic) group equality and or equality in relation to women, sexual orientation or disablement as a strategic issue. Examples relating to poverty and special needs are set out below.

> The City Council works in four areas to help fight poverty:
>
> ■ Working in partnership – working with other agencies to scrutinise and lobby local, regional, national or international organisations to try to ensure that their actions have a positive rather than negative effect on poverty in Norwich.
>
> ■ Helping the economy – trying to ensure ... that people already living in the city get the training and assistance they need to take up available jobs.
>
> ■ Supporting income levels – helping people maintain their income through our own distribution of benefits, charging and debt recovery policies, supporting advice and advocacy centres and by helping community initiatives.
>
> ■ Improving access – to ensure that people's access to services is as equal as possible. This includes removing physical barriers and barriers of cost, caring responsibilities, prejudice and attitudes, transport.
>
> (Norwich City Council)

> To work with other agencies to enable people with special needs to live as full a life as possible within the community, whilst making residential services available where these are appropriate.
>
> (LB Bexley)

Other examples of genuine corporate strategic issues which feature in the local authority documents which have been received are set out below. Most of these are examples of what John Stewart has defined as 'wicked issues' – issues for which there is no simple solution and where no one organisation or agency of government has sole prerogative (Stewart 1995a, p.40).

1. *Environmental sustainability* (often linked to Agenda 21 initiatives):

> To work towards environmental sustainability by, wherever possible, satisfying our current needs whilst not compromising the ability of future generations to satisfy their needs.
>
> (Dudley MBC)

2. *Economic regeneration* – sometimes focusing on a particular developmental project, or the impact of a recent plant closure:

> The council intends to increase its level of involvement in economic development activity and to develop networking and partnerships in order to ensure that the needs of the district are recognised and met. Its main aims will be:
>
> ■ to promote sustainable patterns of economic development and infrastructure, whilst protecting the character and quality of the district's network and built environment;
>
> ■ to build on key sectors in the district's economy – particularly retailing, tourism and farming – in particular to develop sustainable tourism and cultural tourism;
>
> ■ to develop a more active approach to assisting existing firms, particularly small and medium-sized enterprises.
>
> (East Hampshire DC)

3. *Community safety* – a concern about the insecurity felt by increasing numbers of people in and around their homes, related to increases (or, sometimes perceptions of increases) in local crime statistics:

> To help alleviate the fear of crime through working in partnership with key agencies on delivering practical solutions to local problems and to support the police in reducing crime through tackling perceived root causes.
>
> (LB Ealing)

4. *Community health* – sometimes in an educative sense, but sometimes expressed in terms of opposition to a proposal to close a hospital (or a hospital rationalisation):

> The council aims to work in close partnership with the health commission towards a healthier Sunderland, with particular emphasis on improved health awareness, access to health services, accident prevention and greater involvement of its citizens in the making of decisions which affect their health and social welfare.
>
> (Sunderland MBC)

> To ensure that the work of the council makes a positive contribution to promoting the health of Wiltshire people, at county and local levels, in partnership with the Health Commission for Wiltshire and Bath.
>
> (Wiltshire CC)

5. *Traffic control* – reducing the adverse effect of the car on the quality of life (particularly in town centres):

> In Cheltenham and surrounding areas, levels of car ownership and use are high. The result is more accidents, greater pollution and a higher demand for parking space, especially in the town centre. Congestion too is increasing, and can delay business traffic. In Cheltenham with its historic road network and limited resources, solutions are not easy ... we aim to restrain the growth of traffic, particularly by private car ... one important element is the development of a 'Park and Ride' system for Cheltenham ...
>
> (Cheltenham BC)

6. *Resistance to urban encroachment*

> New Forest District, as a quiet place free from pollution, and, set apart from the intensely built-up nearby conurbations, is able strongly to resist harmful growth from regional demands.
>
> (New Forest DC)

7. *The street scene*

> A clean, healthy and well laid-out street scene is important for everybody whether they live in, work in or visit Islington. We will develop a 'partnership for clean streets', and improve other aspects of the street scene.
>
> (LB Islington)

All the above examples of strategic issues have the following characteristics in common.

- They involve areas of concern in which the statutory responsibilities of the council are limited or non-existent.

- They imply action from a number of different service departments, on a co-ordinated basis.

- They typically imply partnership or co-operation with external agencies also or sometimes the application of pressure on external agencies to reconsider proposals.

- They focus on issues which are specific to the authority in question Although issues like environmental sustainability appear on many local authority strategic agendas, the particular nature of the objectives, problems, threats and opportunities will be unique to each authority.

This is not to argue that issues with different characteristics (e.g. service-based statutory responsibilities) may not sometimes be appropriate elements of a strategic agenda. The above list is meant to give a general picture not a set of exclusive criteria!

The components of a strategic issue

A vision statement is perhaps best seen as a strategic agenda – a list of the key issues which an authority wishes to tackle. Although the dominance of 'end-state' objectives in a strategy statement was criticised earlier, there is a place for them on a strategic agenda. A 'safe' clean and pleasant environment, for example, is fine as far as it goes. But what really matters is how committed an authority is to such outcomes and what it intends to do about them. It is only when one moves into the realm of potential action that strategic visions really begin to impinge upon the life of an authority.

To move towards this goal of influential strategies, it is important to balance the 'positive' and 'negative' qualities of strategic issues. The most helpful way of analysing a strategic issue is to regard it as having four components: a desired end state (or, at the very least, a desired direction of change); a conception of the nature of the current problems (which have to be overcome before the end state can be reached); a view of potential threats which may aggravate the problem; and finally a view of the opportunities which exist to resolve the problem and more towards the desired end state.

This model (*see* Fig. 8.1) clearly bears some resemblance to the more familiar SWOT (Strengths, Weaknesses, Opportunities, Threats) analysis. But there is an important difference, SWOT analyses are typically applied internally within the organisation itself. The identification of strategic issues involves, however, an analysis of external circumstances and issues. It asks the question, what is happening out there which will change the nature of the problems it is facing or which may help it to resolve them? Issues of organisational capacity are clearly of crucial importance in developing a response to a strategic agenda: but they are 'second order' issues. The analysis of the strategic issues themselves comes first, irrespective of the organisational capacity to deal with them. The agenda then moves to the requisite organisational change (*see* Chapter 10).

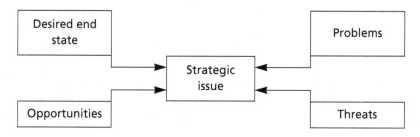

Fig. 8.1 The components of a strategic issue

The requirement to identify the nature of the problem is helpful in two ways. Firstly, problem specification, in relation to a strategic issue, requires a more precise identification of what an authority thinks is detrimental to the quality of life of its residents. What, to continue the 'environmental quality' example, is unsafe, dirty or unpleasant about the authority's existing environment? Is the main concern the danger, noise and pollution from traffic? The legacy of dereliction from the recent history of mining activities? The visual intrusion and air pollution from a large chemical works? The state of the waterways in the authority? Or some combination of these factors?

The second benefit from an emphasis on problems is that it increases the commitment of politicians to the idea and value of 'strategic vision'. Faced with a desired end state type of objective, elected members will often be prepared to endorse it but it will not stimulate their political energy in the way that the identification of a problem will. Responding to problems is a central element of political life, whether the problem is constituent-based (delay over essential repairs), policy-related (a shortage of low-cost housing) or stems from public opposition to the activities of another agency (a hospital closure, for example, or a proposed motorway extension). To focus a debate about strategic issues on problems (in the first instance at least) is to maximise the chances of political involvement. Political commitment is one of the necessary conditions for a strategy to become effective.

The identification of 'threats' may imply either the worsening of an existing problem or the loss of a presently existing valued state. In some cases, statistical analysis of trends may be needed to predict the scale of threat (e.g. changing demographic structure leading to a significant increase in the numbers of the vulnerable elderly; rising trends in particular types of crime). This aspect of strategy is discussed below (pp.97–101). However, as far as possible, the starting point in the identification of threats – as in all aspects of strategic issues – should be by elected members themselves. If they perceive a rising level of concern amongst their constituents about the safety of their local environment, that in itself, is significant, whatever the statistical trend evidence concerning crimes committed.

Opportunities are ways in which new legislation, sources of finance, social change or institutional arrangements may help to contribute towards the solution of the problem.

Environmental quality as a strategic issue

In one of the authorities in which one of the authors has worked, members were exploring 'environmental quality' as a strategic issue. The main problem was perceived by members to be the legacy of dereliction from coal mining and clay working activities in the area. The main threat identified to the desired state of a 'safe and clean and pleasant environment' was the set of development pressures for housing, roads, and support services which would be generated by the expansion of a large car manufacturing plant within the authority's boundaries. This event in fact highlighted another dimension of strategic choice: the inter-relationship between strategic issues. The expansion of the car manufacturing plant was viewed by members as an opportunity in relation to another strategic issue

– economic self-sufficiency – in which there was a strong commitment to the outcome of 'no net outward migration in relation to journey-to-work' in the authority. The expansion of the car manufacturing plant would clearly contribute to this outcome, while at the same time making the achievement of a 'safe clean and pleasant environment' more difficult. The choices implied by this interaction, are in a very real sense, what strategic planning is all about.

The key opportunity identified in relation to environmental quality in this authority was the fact that a significant part of its territory was shortly to be designated as part of the National Forest, with the potential for further expansion in due course. In other circumstances, SRB projects or grants from the National Lottery might constitute the main opportunity for moving towards a desired state.

A strategy for empowerment

This strategic agenda does not come from a specific local authority: it has been drawn up by the authors as illustrative of the way in which a key issue, once identified may be broken down into a number of specific components.

As a public sector organisation does the council represent and empower the community and its component parts? The best way to ensure the public is served is by ensuring the public is fully represented, through:

1. elections – and other forms of democracy (e.g. see Stewart 1995a);

2. demographic composition of council (members and officers);

3. composition at different levels and in different parts of the organisation which differ in function, status, power and rewards;

4. service delivery and the allocation of services (both 'positive' helping and 'negative' controlling services);

5. cost sharing and the allocation of cost, through taxes and service charges.

Assumptions

1. People find it hard to relate to problems they have not experienced – therefore build a range of experience into the organisation.

2. What steps are being taken to get there? Positive action and community development will be needed.

3. Admit that there is racism/sexism/other kinds of discrimination/inequality in the community and the council.

4. Train people within the council to recognise, and to deal with these issues.

5. Monitor results in each dimension.

Trend analysis and strategic scenarios

Strategic planning is by definition concerned with looking ahead. Although strategic priorities may be rooted in the perception of current problems (e.g. the sudden collapse of the basic industry of the locality) the other components of a strategic issue – threats, opportunities and desired end states (or vision) are explicitly future-oriented. A desired end state requires the forward-looking exercise of imagination to picture what an area could be like if particular impediments were removed or problems resolved. The analysis of both threats and opportunities must necessarily move beyond those that exist at present (the availability of Lottery grants, the completion of a new stretch of motorway) to those which might develop in the future. In this context, trend analysis and forecasting become important potential contributions to understanding and planning. If there is concern about the alienation and anti-social activities of unemployed young people, is the problem likely to increase or decrease in the future? The answer to this question implies both demographic and employment availability trend data. If there is concern about the problems of the single parent family, then demographic trends and marriage stability trends are both relevant. A concern with traffic congestion requires an understanding of car ownership and usage pattern trends. Readers can no doubt readily supplement this list with their own examples.

There are now a number of agencies which specialise in the analysis of social and economic trends of this nature. The Henley Centre, for example, produce reports on a regular basis setting out and analysing such forecasts. The most recent exercise (LGMB 1997) highlighted, inter alia, the following trends.

1. *Economic internationalisation* involving the increasing mobility of capital and investment across national boundaries and involving a shift in power to the Pacific Rim and Asian economies.

2. *Fragmentation* of economic enterprise and work opportunities, of the family and social structure and (although the report does not stress this fact) of the responsibility for local service provision.

3. *Polarisation* of occupational structure, income, employment security and residential territory between the 30 per cent of adults in secure well-paid jobs and the 40 per cent living below or close to the margins of poverty.

4. *Increased mobility* in relation to car-ownership and use, residence, and career patterns (except for the bottom 40 per cent).

5. *Increased participation/activism* in relation to personal grievances, environmental issues, and locality defence (but not in the industrial relations field).

6. *Equalisation of opportunities* in relation to employment, career development and life style, between women and men.

The relevance of this kind of trend analysis to local authority corporate agendas is well illustrated by a paper which draws out the implications of these trends for local government (Leach and Hall 1997). The paper argues that we are likely to see:

- increased demand for nursery school places (and child-minding facilities generally) as more women with children under five become economically active;

- new challenges in the strategic role of managing housing demand as pressure for more small-unit housing accommodation increases;

- problems of managing surplus capacity in the primary education sector, and coping with growing demand in secondary education;

- increasing pressure for imaginative traffic regulation schemes to minimise the undesirable effects of the private use of the car;

- the increasing demand for leisure/recreational facilities (public and private) particularly in the fast growing 55–64 age group;

- more early retirements which could also provide the opportunity for more people to become involved in their local communities.

However, the problem of trend analysis on a national or even regional basis, is that it cannot – except in broad terms – be applied directly to local scenarios. What is important locally is the particular interplay of local circumstances and national trends, and the impact of specific local scenarios. Thus the potential impact of IT developments on office location and employment levels will clearly be more profound in some areas than others. This means that a local authority-specific interpretation process is necessary, to inter-relate national trends and local circumstances and aspirations.

Many local authorities, in their strategy documents, are adept enough at identifying and taking account of future demographic changes in population size and distribution, household size and sometimes socio-economic composition. Economic and employment trends are also often addressed, although with the acknowledgement of the greater degree of uncertainty involved and the presumption that the local authority can itself affect such trends. The attempt to interpret the overall impact locally of different social, economic and environmental trends is rarely attempted. One particularly impressive example of an authority which has attempted to do so is Epsom and Ewell DC. Their recent draft report 'A Strategic Framework for Epsom and Ewell' is worth examining at some length. The analysis will illustrate the radical nature of the changes involved, and the inter-relationships between them.

The document recognises that 'we live in a period of unparalleled economic, social and technological change'. It identifies four dominant themes:

- economic uncertainty, as a result of changing employment patterns;

- governments continuing to find it difficult to finance their activities;

- wider gaps between 'haves' and 'have nots';

- advances in information technology.

Amongst the implications with a significant level of potential impact on the Epsom and Ewell area are the following.

- Offices, which employ over 40 per cent of local people, will be automated, and advances in communications will make geographical location of offices increasingly irrelevant.

- Many clerical, secretarial and management jobs (in which some 60 per cent of local people are employed) are likely to be lost.

- More people will be employed on short-term contracts, where security of employment and benefits will often be less.

- Cost pressures will mean that many jobs are part-time rather than full-time. More people will have more than one job.

- Up to 30 per cent of workers may be based at home on a given day, with a smaller number working at home most of the time.

- Those without marketable skills are likely to find life increasingly difficult as state aid diminishes. Anti-social behaviour, crime and security will continue to be high profile issue.

- Increased home-working may lead to a break-up of the main commuter flows and the growth of more diverse journey patterns. This could have an adverse effect on public transport viability.

- The disappearance of marginal shops and shopping areas will continue. Many banks or other high street institutions are likely to close.

The important quality of the Epsom and Ewell Strategic Framework document is that it attempts to highlight the cumulative impact of these changes on the local authority area and its resident population, and begins to identify ways in which the council could respond to the threats and opportunities posed by this change agenda. The report recognises that as many more activities are enabled by technology to locate anywhere, then they will choose lower cost locations, few of which are likely to be in South East England. There is, therefore, a risk of the borough becoming less favoured than it has been in the past. There is a threat to economic viability of the town centre, reflecting the decline of offices, marginal shops and shopping areas, and banks and other 'high street' financial institutions. The Strategic Framework document details a number of possible policy responses, for example, to identify 'core areas' where retail use will be protected; to facilitate the preservation of a minimum core of local convenience outlets; and to take action to enhance the social value of shopping trips. Many of these impacts are of course by no means specific to Epsom and Ewell. The particular value of the report lies in its ability to make links between changing economic structure, journey patterns, environmental issues, and the viability of the main retail centre in the area. It represents too, a pioneering attempt to inter-relate trend analysis, local circumstances and policy responses and demonstrates the relevance of longer-term strategic analysis.

But perhaps the most encouraging feature of the report is what it says about local citizenship. The report makes an important link between the economic restructuring scenario and a second strategic issue – the challenge for local authorities of enhancing their legitimacy with local people. The Strategic Framework argues that one of the unanticipated consequences of the economic restructuring which is forecast could be to encourage citizenship and community spirit.

Home working, more expensive travel and less assured incomes all point to a world where more people spend more time in their immediate neighbourhood. This could give rise to a greater sense of community, more participation in voluntary activity and a greater concern with the quality of local facilities of all types. Early retirement could provide more opportunity for more people to become involved in their local community. New ways of communication will make it easier for local people to participate in community affairs.

Effective active citizenship requires that participatory arrangements are stronger and more efficient . . . The Borough Council is well-placed to broker these arrangements, but would defeat the purpose if it sought to dominate them.

This is an outcome which could be of considerable potential benefit for local authorities, if they can demonstrate both a receptiveness to the strengthening forces of community spirit and citizenship, and an ability to broker and channel these forces into positive outcomes. In so doing authorities could provide both an invaluable resource for meeting their own strategic agendas and experience a strengthening of the community loyalty so crucial to the future health of local government.

The future of strategic visions

As was demonstrated in Chapter 2 more and more authorities are adopting a community governance role (*see* Clarke and Stewart 1990). They are identifying local needs and priorities and taking action to deal with them, above and beyond any statutory responsibilities. They are acting on the voice of their local community. Interestingly there is a proposal in the most recent Labour Party policy document on local government (Labour Party 1995) which would have the effect of strengthening this kind of local authority activity.

We suggest that Parliament places on councils a duty to promote the overall social and economic well-being of the communities they serve. In parallel, councils could be given a new power of community initiative to respond to local needs.

Some of the content of a strategic vision will reflect the content of a party manifesto. Other elements are more likely to emerge as political priorities during the term of office of a majority party or coalition. The important point to stress here is the inter-relationship between party priorities, community governance and strategic visions.

Taking the strategic agenda forward

In this chapter, we have discussed the appropriate composition of corporate strategic agendas and identified what kind of issues are appropriate for inclusion, and why. Many of the strategic documents we received in connection with this book comprised of or included short summaries of strategic issues of this nature. It is important to stress, on the basis of what has already been written in this chapter, that to form the basis for effective action (and for transforming the decision-making processes of the authority), the strategic agenda should possess the following characteristics:

1. political commitment/ownership;

2. a predominance of non-service-specific issues (i.e. issues which reflect a commitment to community governance in the wider sense);

3. either a limited number of strategic issues (five or six at most) or a clear sense of prioritisation amongst a larger number;

4. a conception of the issue which goes beyond a statement of long-term objectives and includes a view of the nature of the problem or problems to be addressed and also ideally an outline of likely threats and opportunities;

5. some preliminary exploration of the inter-relationship between the strategic issues identified.

For an authority which wishes to emphasise service issues and is less concerned to address a wider strategic agenda, a corporate strategy would take a different and more limited form.

It could:

■ place different priorities on individual services (for example, protect education and social services, if necessary at the expense of recreation and highways) or on elements of services (under fives, the schools budget, children at risk);

■ develop a strategy which is based on bids by services committees/ departments for developments which they see as positive and which the council then subjects to critical scrutiny and from which it develops a select list. The outcome may then provide indications as to a set of more general principles, which can be used in subsequent strategy formulation exercises.

But the development of a strategic agenda, although a crucial first stage in establishing a planning process, is only a first stage. The subsequent challenge is to:

- carry out more systematic analysis on the strategic issues identified and the inter-relationship between them;

- develop action proposals for addressing these issues;

- set up appropriate organisational machinery (formal and informal) for taking forward the strategic planning process;

- develop process proposals which will build the strategic agenda into the cycle of council activities in a systematic way (typically labelled as policy planning processes or medium-term planning systems);

- clarify the links between the strategic planning process and the budgetary process;

- develop a monitoring process to establish in due course how effective the strategy is proving.

It is important, in the first instance, not to swamp the initial political process of the identification of strategic issues – which is the element which stimulates the most enthusiasm, and can 'kick-start' the whole initiative – with these more prosaic details of structure and process. But once the commitment is established and an initial issues statement develops, it is necessary to move on to such detail. It is at this stage also that a recognition of the potential sources of resistance to a corporate strategy becomes important. The development of such a strategy, if it is effective, will re-allocate financial resources and statuses within the authority. It is thus not a politically 'neutral' endeavour which will command widespread support. It will be viewed by some organisational interests as threats and by others as opportunities. It is through such a potential minefield that the strategic initiative must be steered. Chapters 5 and 6 addressed these issues.

> It is important not to swamp the initial political process of the identification of strategic issues with the more prosaic details of structure and process.

SUMMARY

- Strategic agendas work most effectively in the following circumstances:

    (i) political commitment/ownership;

(ii) a predominance of non-service-specific issues (i.e. issues which reflect a commitment to community governance in the wider sense);

(iii) either a limited number of strategic issues (five or six at most) or a clear sense of prioritisation amongst a larger number;

(vi) a conception of the issue which goes beyond a statement of long-term objectives and includes a view of the nature of the problem or problems to be addressed and (ideally also an outline of likely threats and opportunities);

(v) some preliminary exploration of the inter-relationship between the strategic issues identified.

- Service-specific issues should be included in corporate strategic agendas only if they have such major repercussions for the service concerned (e.g. the voluntary role of the council housing stock) that they become 'de facto' corporate issues.

- The use of trend analysis and social and economic forecasting is helpful as a stimulus to think about how a local authority is likely to change, i.e. the threats and opportunities which are implied for the authority's strategic agenda.

- Strategic agendas should be reviewed on a regular basis. Typically it would be expected that some strategic issues would move off a strategic agenda, and other new ones move on as circumstances change.

9

Corporate strategies and council budgets

INTRODUCTION

In this chapter we consider the significance of council budgets and budget setting for the development of corporate strategies. The chapter begins by considering the contemporary financial climate for local authorities in Britain and the ways in which heightened fiscal pressures have increased the significance and difficulty of budgetary decisions. It then examines the relationship between budgets and strategies, and suggests how this relationship must be developed in order to strengthen a strategic approach. Alternative principles of budget setting are examined, including the difference between incremental and priority based budgets. The chapter concludes by considering the methods by which the potentially divisive process of prioritisation and budget setting can be managed by members and officers.

The financial climate

Since the 1970s it has become orthodox opinion in governing circles that the level of state provision and state expenditure in Britain has grown too high and can no longer be afforded. In these circumstances central government has been particularly concerned to devise ways of containing those components of public spending which are 'demand-led' (as in the case of unemployment and social security benefits) or controlled by independent agencies (such as local councils). This concern also, however, coincided with and was fuelled by Conservative government hostility towards public spending that was undertaken by local Labour Parties which constitute part of the political opposition. A sequence of measures has therefore been introduced to centralise control over local authority taxing and spending (starting with the Local Government Planning and Land Act 1980) and to sensitise the local electorate to these issues (through, for example, the ill-fated Poll Tax) in order to induce greater fiscal discipline.

Central controls upon local authority finances apply both to income and expenditure: Standard Spending Assessments control global and service block spending; universal capping criteria restrict the tax varying powers of councils to within a certain range; and the National Non-domestic Rate takes control over business rates away from local authorities. Since 1989 local authority finances have been squeezed hard, and this has been accomplished in good part by transferring the source of council revenues from localities themselves to central government, leaving only about fifteen per cent of local authority net revenue funding to be collected locally. One consequence is that in 1991/92, for example, about 35,000 full-time and 11,000 part-time jobs were lost from local government (Pinch 1995, p.969). At the same time, however, expenditure by central government upon national quangos and agencies in localities (UDCs, Task Forces, TECs and even local regeneration partnerships involving local authorities but funded through City Challenge or the Single Regeneration Budget) has grown dramatically. The squeeze on local authority resources has made allocative decisions within councils much more important and difficult than before, and has induced many councils to look for better and more strategic ways of making budget cuts, and of limiting the ensuing damage to the organisation, its goals and relationships. Budget planning has been strengthened in order to:

- maximise what discretion the local authority, its members and officers have over the allocation of scarce resources between service heads;

- begin planning difficult decisions early in order to avoid unwelcome surprises late in the financial year, surprises that will add to pain and conflict;

- take hold of important cross-committee and cross-agency decisions before these slip out of reach;

- question the compartmentalisation of sectional or departmental budgets;

- provide a basis for budget decisions that is reasonable and can command widespread support by reference to stated values and priorities;

- devise a process that will enable a consensus to be formed between leading members and officers;

- extend involvement in budget decisions and 'ownership' of these (with all their attendant difficulties) across the key members of a political coalition;

- sound out and prepare public opinion, and manage unforeseen implications through expedients such as the creation of a reserve fund;

- respond to new management thinking with its emphasis upon devolved, cash limited budgets, performance management, and service quality.

It is unfortunate but perhaps inevitable that innovations in budget setting should have developed in response to fiscal pressures rather than to the growth of council budgets. Over recent years local authorities have been placed in the unenviable position of having to demonstrate their competence and secure their viability by devising ever more effective ways of pruning budgets and of handling the destructive consequences of this process for local political and professional relationships. There is a danger that the genuine achievements which have been made in this field (and which are discussed below) will make us forget that the present climate for local government, with the reduction of the powers and resources of local democratically elected bodies, is neither desirable nor inevitable.

The relationship between strategies and budgets

Corporate strategies can influence what a council does in a number of different ways.

- They can change the ways in which services are provided, their quality, distribution, effectiveness, efficiency and co-ordination.

- They can change the level of resources devoted to each service and the distribution of resources between services.

- They can change the way in which services are paid for, as between taxes, service charges and grants.

A key issue in the development of a strategic approach to corporate management (whether in public or private sectors) is the relationship which is established between organisational objectives and financial resources. The ability to determine the allocation of resources between activities according to the requirements of corporate priorities is a necessary condition for effective strategic management. In order to explore these issues further we must, however, begin by being realistic about the complexity of the relationships here.

1. The strategies and priorities that can be pursued by a council (or any organisation) are always affected by budgetary limitations that are fixed in the short term – all strategies are necessarily *budgetarily constrained*. These limitations may derive from the tax preferences of the local community, from central government controls, from the elasticity of demand for services, or from a combination of these factors. It is no use adopting priorities that cannot be accommodated within the existing budget, although steps may be taken to change these limitations for the medium and longer term.

2. Most corporate strategies are at least in part *resource maximising* in the sense that they seek to protect councils' structures and staff by giving priority to activities that can attract funding from other sources. Sources of funding include central government (e.g. City Challenge and the SRB Challenge Fund), the European Union (e.g. European Structure Funds) or other agencies (e.g. the National Lottery). Self-preservation must always be one component of a council's strategy, although there is a danger that under certain conditions it will become an over-riding concern.

3. Some corporate strategies may be geared directly and specifically to the overall level of the council's taxes and expenditure, and are therefore *fiscally centred*. A number of authorities emphasise cost reduction and tax minimisation, for example, while others emphasise service maximisation by raising taxes as high as is politically acceptable (on this distinction *see* for example Pinch 1995). In the former case it will be argued that the public good is benefited most by encouraging personal responsibility and private provision; in the latter case it will be argued that the market by itself will benefit the strong at the expense of the weak and must therefore be balanced by public provision.

All council strategies are budgetarily constrained, most will be resource maximising, and most will take a position somewhere between the extremes of tax minimising and service maximising. But if strategic management is to be effective then a more positive relationship must be established between strategies and budgets, such that council objectives not only reflect budgetary considerations but also help to influence these considerations and the allocation of resources between activities. All too often while budgetary considerations exercise a clear influence upon strategic decisions, there is no clear chain of causation running the other way, from the council's corporate strategy to its corporate budget. This situation may arise because:

- there may be no agreed corporate strategy, or no strategy with the clarity and the backing required to exert a real influence upon the corporate budget;

- no method may have been devised for linking the strategy to the budget in an acceptable way at the corporate level;

- corporate budget setting may be viewed as a routine process that continues unexamined from one year to the next, or as a technical process that can only be handled by experts, or as a political process that must be undertaken by a small cabal away from strategic or policy considerations;

- political and managerial strategies may exert an influence upon budget allocations primarily at the committee or departmental level, where resources are moved around more readily in response to priorities established by members and officers.

Clearly the budget process is a central focus for the expression of vested organisational interests, and it will therefore be difficult to change the ways in which budgets are set, or to make this process more transparent. Corporate strategies can still be valuable and important even when they do not have a direct impact upon the budget, helping to imbue activities across the council with a similar style and emphasis. Indeed local authorities are not alone in finding it difficult to relate budgets to strategies: 'the translation between strategies and budgets' is also a blind spot in private sector strategic management (Mintzberg 1994, p.74). But

> **Local authorities are not alone in finding it difficult to relate budgets to strategies.**

financially detached strategies will find that they are operating alongside an implicit 'strategy' or set of corporate priorities that have been embedded in the budget structure over the years and are carried forward as a de facto 'budget-based strategy'. The challenge for councils is therefore to find effective and durable ways of reflecting corporate strategies in budgetary decisions, and of overcoming the power of the implicit strategy that is embodied in the budget and that remains unquestioned from one year to the next.

Incremental versus priority based budgets

A contrast is often drawn between two broad approaches to budget setting, incremental budgeting and priority based budgeting (e.g. CIPFA 1990). *Incremental budgeting* involves taking the overall structure of this year's base budget as given and considering bids for incremental increases or reductions on a service by service basis for next financial year. Although traditional in local government, this approach has certain drawbacks which have become more important as resources have been squeezed. In particular, focusing on individual items of expenditure detracts attention from overall priorities between broad areas of service. *Priority based budgeting,* on the other hand, involves the preparation of a strategic plan and priority listing which then guides budget decisions. As well as focusing debate on the global allocation of resources between committees rather than individual items of expenditure, this approach allows members and directors to set overall priorities to inform this global allocation. It permits the delegation of budgetary control to cost centres, giving managers more control over their own resources. Alternative versions of priority based budgeting include:

- the Policy Programme Budgeting Systems applied to US military expenditure in the 1960s, which 'represented a formal attempt to couple strategic planning with programming and budgeting in a single system' (Mintzberg 1994, p.117);

- Zero Based Budgeting whereby the existing components of the budget are swept away and regenerated at regular intervals to ensure they are not included through inertia but reflect agreed organisational objectives;

- Base Budget Review which involves a re-examination of the base budget in the light of council priorities without pretending this base can be swept away at regular intervals.

The strengths and weaknesses of the incremental and priority approaches to budgets can be compared as follows (*see* CIPFA 1990):

	Strengths	Weaknesses
Incremental	Simple	Budget not linked to strategy
	Inexpensive	Focus on the margins
		Cuts are arbitrary
Priority based	Budget is linked to strategy	Time-consuming
	Looks at the whole budget	Laborious
	Participative	

However, whatever its attractions, few if any authorities have in practice used priority based budgeting in its pure form – starting from scratch each year – and those instances which can be identified have generally happened at the committee level (e.g. Roberts and Scholes 1993). The existing base budget reflects the impact of accumulated experience and pressures over many years. It reflects statutory duties and other practical obligations which have been embodied in various capital assets, staff resources, contracts and service commitments. It cannot, therefore, be swept away without causing considerable damage in the process. But the base budget should not be regarded as sacrosanct; it may not coincide very closely with current circumstances, nor with agreed manifesto commitments or strategic priorities, nor with public needs or expectations. It is for these reasons that the base budget must be re-examined, especially during periods of rapid change.

It can therefore be anticipated that priority based budgeting will usually be introduced in a qualified, partial or selective manner such that incrementation will be modified by an infusion of some form of priority based budgeting. Where budgets are prepared according to policy priorities they will in most cases also be prepared incrementally, starting with last year's expenditure commitments rather than a blank sheet of paper. There may be occasional reviews of the base budget, or parts of this, along with a prioritisation exercise, but the end result will still in most cases be a marginal adjustment to existing

> **Priority based budgeting will usually be introduced in a qualified, partial or selective manner.**

budgetary allocations. The result will be a hybrid approach in which priorities are applied by a variety of means to last year's base budget in order to recognise the council's existing commitments whilst accommodating members' desire to protect certain services above others (Collinge and Leach 1995).

Furthermore, while budget setting must be planned and programmed it is unwise to exaggerate the capacity of local government – or any large organisation – for behaviour which is rational in the formal sense, which starts with a strategic plan and deduces priorities, budgets and service levels. Budget-setting – especially in a political context – is always likely to be to some degree fuzzy and incremental, in some or all of the following ways:

- involving political considerations and non-policy priorities that are not necessarily spelled out in making budget allocations;

- involving iteration – checking the budgetary implications of policy priorities before the latter are settled;

- involving indeterminacy in the links between policy priorities and budget decisions – it is no simple matter to derive budgetary implications from policy priorities.

Existing organisational structures – such as committees and departments and the interests they support – are bound to be reflected within budgets and to exert a predominantly conservative influence upon budget decisions.

The management of strategic budgeting

There are many different ways in which councils have attempted to introduce and manage a strategic approach to budget setting. The following describes the processes in terms of which attempts are made to introduce this kind of approach.

The planning of budget setting

The link between budget setting and strategy may be part of a formal policy planning or corporate management process operating on an annual cycle. This process may involve only leading members and officers, or chairs of committees and all chief officers. Broad budgetary guidelines may be established in May or June of each year, in the light of forecasts regarding the probable range within which the settlement will fall, indicating the position to be taken on the council tax, reserves, pay awards, demographic and statutory changes.

The formulation of priorities

The statement of priorities is a necessary step in the development of the budget implications of strategy. Priorities may be formulated proactively and set down in advance of budget options, or they may be invoked in response to budget options. In other words, the process of budget setting can be used to clarify the council's strategic priorities. In practice it is likely that both approaches will be involved in a circular or interactive process. Some councils may go so far as to check their service or budgetary priorities with the public by, for instance, conducting a public opinion survey. Council priorities may take the form of simple broad statements (for instance that direct services have higher priority than support services, or that education be given the highest priority over the next three years), or they may involve detailed lists of service areas arranged in priority order that indicates their budgetary position. Once again each approach has its merits and a council must select a method that is suited to its experience and culture. In some cases councils have attached a numerical weight to different services allowing a direct link to be made with budget changes.

The link between strategic priorities and the budget

The link between priorities and the budget may be loose and organic – for instance with differential percentage cuts between support and direct services – or tied very closely to services – for instance, by scoring service areas or even using computer modelling and decision support systems. Overall budgets for committees may be the result, or members may go further and set detailed budgets within committees and departments. This link may be made through a voting system, or a star chamber in which bids from committees are interrogated.

In practice political realignment (perhaps brought on by shifting electoral fortunes) and currents of opinion in local communities and amongst members and other opinion formers (such as the media) can lead to new strategic priorities which are reflected very directly in the council's budget. This happened in Birmingham in the early 1980s, for example, when the emphasis was placed upon city centre redevelopment and prestige schemes in order to combat the sense of decline that had arisen during the depths of the first Thatcher recession (1979–83). It happened once again in Birmingham in the early 1990s, when there was a reaction against the run down of school facilities, which led to spending above SSA on the education block.

Budgets in which there are priorities involve winners and losers, and are therefore politically controversial and difficult to establish. In situations of political continuity, budgets can be guided by simple rules of thumb (such as 'protecting front line services', 'protecting education and social services', 'protecting statutory duties'). Sometimes this can go further, and very specific priorities will be developed in terms of services, perhaps using various decision support techniques and voting mechanisms, as happened in Sandwell and in Dudley in the early 1990s. Finally, it is possible for fairly subtle and detailed priority based budgets to be developed, in which money is moved between committees and in which overall cuts are combined with growth in specific areas, through negotiation and debate in a non-mechanical vein. Perhaps it is this method, relying as it does upon political debate rather than rule of thumb or decision support techniques, which reflects the greatest political skill and maturity.

Some of the different ways in which budgets may be guided by strategies are as follows:

- political re-alignments reflected in new budget priorities;
- changing currents of local public opinion (and their manipulation) impacting upon budget planning;

- simple rules of thumb (such as protecting front line services);
- use of mechanical prioritisation techniques;
- priorities negotiated and agreed through informed political debate.

Efficiency considerations

A decision about policy priorities need not determine the budgetary outcome directly, but may be related first to efficiency considerations. Even if a service is a high priority its budget might be considered to be slack, or to contain areas of inefficiency that should be removed. Sometimes this is based upon a gut feeling, but sometimes specific evidence exists of overspending on, for example, administration or on vacancies. Comparators within and between councils (such as audit profiles) might be used in this context.

Decision support systems

Decision conferencing is a method of budget setting which uses a facilitated workshop involving computer modelling, and enables comparisons to be made between different patterns of service provision and resource allocation. The first step is for committee chairs or departmental managers to consider each of their cost centres in turn and to identify the service implications of, for example, seven incremental changes in the expenditure on this service as follows:

+15%   +10%   +5%   +0%   −5%   −10%   −15%

If this is done for each of (say) the 10 cost centres within the department then 70 different service/budget options will be identified, options which will then be entered into a computer. A decision conferencing session would then take place within each department or committee to construct committee level service/budget options. Once again these might be set at the same seven different levels of expenditure:

+15%   +10%   +5%   +0%   −5%   −10%   −15%

These committee options would be built up by permutating different cost centre options – increases in some areas, reductions in others – to give combinations which provide the greatest overall benefit available at seven different levels of committee expenditure. Explicit criteria are required in order to compare the benefits to be derived from increasing or reducing expenditure on services. These criteria can be derived from pre-existing statements of objectives that have already been agreed, or they can be generated through debate during the conference. The sort of criteria used include 'quality of service', 'equality', 'image', 'electability'. These criteria are used by the participants at the committee level conference to score service/budget packages on a preference scale between 0 and 100. When the results of the debate are fed into the computer this allows a comparison to be made between the different options in terms of all the criteria combined. It also allows these (and the existing pattern of spending) to be compared to the optimum cost/benefit package of services and spending by showing where they fall on a graph of cost against benefit. The relative importance of different criteria can also be taken into account by weighting these differently.

The results at the committee level could then be taken forward to the corporate level. Once again a decision conference would be held in which the participants (corporate members and officers) were asked to decide the relative merits of the service/budget options for each committee, and to choose a combination of these that gives the maximum overall benefit according to criteria that are brought into, or generated from, the discussion. A decision conference is a two day event which involves a facilitator and computer operator provided for a price by a firm of computer consultants. The ideal number of participants for a conference is between 7 and 15 people. Decision conferencing has a number of strengths. It involves the use of agreed criteria against which services will be ranked, and allows different weights to be attached to these criteria. It allows a comparison to be made between the existing pattern of service provision and the optimum pattern at the same level of expenditure. It permits a form of zero based budgeting, identifying the services that would be put in place if the council was starting without existing commitments. It involves the preparation of a range of service centre spending options, so people can see in advance the likely service level implications of broader budgetary decisions. It allows weights and priorities to be shifted quickly showing how these changes affect the allocation of resources.

On the other hand, it also has some weaknesses. It relies on the accuracy of the service centre options, and assumes that managers will not be tempted to exaggerate the likely impact of budget reductions on the council or the community. At the corporate level it compares whole committee budgets with one another, and does not deal separately with the service centres they contain and the priority that may be attached corporately to these individually. By centralising decisions over committee budget options it tends to go against the delegation of budgetary control to committees. It is costly to operate, involving considerable amounts of officer and member time together with a significant charge by the consultants. It becomes less effective if the number of people directly involved exceeds ten, and if people are included without a direct interest in the outcome. It may be that this system is better suited to committee level than corporate level decision making. Some councils, for example Dudley, have however used this to prepare corporate as well as committee budgets, and have found the experience to be a positive and useful way of clarifying issues, raising fundamental budget questions, and converting priorities into budget options.

One approach to priority based budgeting

An example of priority based budgeting is provided by Sandwell Metropolitan Borough Council (much of what follows draws upon Noble and Collinge 1993). Since 1990 Sandwell has been attempting to use its corporate strategy to inform budget setting, to move beyond purely incremental budgeting, and has developed a planning process and budget setting techniques that have enabled it to shift resources between, as well as within, committees. Well before the beginning of each financial year, at a 'policy planning seminar' in June, members and directors meet to review the council's corporate strategy, to establish budgetary guidelines and to review the process for establishing committee targets. The council's corporate strategy sets out a vision of the future to which the organisation aspires, while its budgetary guidelines involve a set of basic decisions – such as the approach to council tax increases and the forecast RSG settlement – which provide a framework for committee target setting. The process of establishing priority based committee budgets, including the role of service prioritisation, is also agreed and a series of policy planning seminars is programmed.

In 1991/92 it was agreed after some discussion that priorities were needed which allowed a ranking of services between – not just within – departments. For the purpose of performance management all departments had already been divided into service centres and the cost of these identified. In the first year of prioritisation (for the 1992–93 budget) members were sent a questionnaire during the summer of 1991 containing a list of the council's 180 service areas with explanatory notes, and were asked to select about 25 per cent of these as having top priority in terms of the council's corporate strategy. The prioritisation questionnaire produced a high response rate – 37 out of 51 members (73 per cent) of the majority group completed the form – and while votes were distributed widely there was a good measure of consensus over the higher and lower priority services. Service areas were then divided by the Policy Unit into four priority bands according to the proportion of members voting for each, and this outcome was presented to a policy planning seminar in August. A number of anomalies were corrected and the resulting rank order was presented to policy and resources committee and the full council in September.

Directors were then asked to identify a total level of savings for their departments reflecting the priority given to the services under their control. In calculating this total it was assumed that services in different priority bands would incur different sized reductions as follows:

higher priority	0%
higher/medium priority	3%
lower/medium priority	9%
lower priority	12%

These percentages were chosen to ensure the total reduction that was required in the overall budget would be achieved, to avoid reducing higher priority services at all, and to produce steeper cuts in services down the priority ladder without cutting them excessively. Within these totals, however, directors were able to use their discretion to arrive at committee budgets and a package of savings which they considered viable.

Needless to say this approach was far from uncontroversial, and encountered a number of difficulties. In particular, it was generally regarded as too complex and mechanical, and did not do much to help members fully to understand the services they were selecting. As the results were the aggregate of all Labour members' preferences they did not necessarily coincide with the views of the political leadership and the requirements of coalition maintenance. Nevertheless, over a period of time the management team developed a package of budget reductions – totalling more than £13 million net, but also including growth of more than £1m – that was guided directly by members' priorities. In preparing for the 1993–94 budget, several improvements were made which attempted to remove some of these difficulties. The number of service centres for members to consider through prioritisation was reduced from 180 to 81 by:

■ removing ring-fenced and non-target services from the exercise;

■ using the client-side to determine priority for contracted services;

- re-allocating the cost of administrative services over the services they support;

- considering in-house services which the council provides to itself (all those recharged to service departments) on block and reducing them by the average reduction.

The 81 services to be prioritised were listed on a form, together with a short description of the service actually provided, an indication of their gross cost and statutory status, and this time a scale from 0 to 10 on which they could be ranked. Once again the scores from returned forms were added up, giving a total for each service centre which was then combined with the cost of the centre to give the budget reduction it would in principle receive. Unlike the previous year the introduction of arbitrary percentages was avoided by using the service centre score and cost to directly calculate its share of the total saving (of more than £11m net) required by the council. The reductions for the services within each committee were then added together to give the revised target for each committee.

This time more than 80 per cent of the members of the majority group responded, and the opposition agreed to use the process to produce an alternative budget. The council did not intend service priorities to be adhered to rigidly by chairs and directors in preparing detailed committee budgets, or to remove delegated financial responsibility from committees. Indeed, the resulting budgets were based on a series of decisions of which prioritisation was only one. Nevertheless, a comparison between priorities and eventual committee estimates for 1992–93 show that prioritisation did indeed guide budget decision making for 1992–93, without determining this in every particular or removing responsibility from chairs or directors for committee budgets. This system had a number of strengths. It enabled members for the first time to spell out their political priorities in concrete terms, matching specific service areas to the council's corporate strategy. It was relatively straightforward, allowing people to understand where priorities had come from. It was democratic and robust and reflected all the opinions of the ruling group.

An alternative approach to priority based budgeting

In the 1980s Kirklees had for much of the time been a hung council, and had managed to establish very little in the way of a common approach to budget setting between the different political groupings. Between 1989 and 1994 however, there was Labour Party majority control and a considerable strengthening of the corporate management and budget-setting processes. This period is, in particular, marked by a close alliance between the Labour leader John Harman and the Council Chief Executive Robert Hughes. One of the first actions of the new Labour administration was to reform the departmental structure, producing a more corporate approach that was also reflected in the committee system, with the appointment of an executive board of elected members from the ruling group. In 1989 the budget process in Kirklees was essentially incremental, with bids and savings being put forward by departments to the Director of Finance for consideration for inclusion in the subsequent annual budget. As usual in these situations the focus of debate was around the marginal changes in the form of spending bids and savings.

In order to create a more strategic approach, corporate budgets based upon planning totals were introduced, together with a process referred as 'skewing'. Planning totals were prepared by departments in the context of an overall figure provided from the centre by the finance department, and were related to a statement of service provision that could be met by this 'base' budget. These planning totals were allocated not for whole areas of service but for specific services, of which 100 were identified across the council, and the totals were 'skewed' according to various criteria that were identified centrally. A seminar had been held each year between the Labour group and District Labour Party towards the end of September in order to indicate to the council leadership what priorities should be adopted and which services should be protected. The 'skewing' of targets or planning totals also took account of changes in service demand, perhaps reflecting demographic change, new legislation, efficiency considerations but also policy priorities derived from the corporate strategy, and under the guidance of the members Budget Review Group. This group together with the whole Labour group also controlled the level of spending in relation to the capping limit, and the size of the council tax and the use of balances.

SUMMARY

There are a number of specific observations with practical relevance that can be drawn out of the preceding discussion.

■ Budget planning is important in order to protect the discretion of local councils, to avoid unwelcome surprises later in the year, to build a consensus behind difficult decisions, and to change the distribution of resources as needs and local circumstances change.

- The relationship between budgets and strategies is bound to be complex: all strategies are budgetarily constrained at least in the short term; most strategies are resource maximising to some degree; and some budgets are centred upon taxation issues (fiscally centred) either seeking to minimise or to maximise council expenditure.

- One of the biggest challenges for local authorities is to find an effective way of reflecting corporate priorities in budgetary decisions and embodying these in the structure of the budget.

- In particular, councils will want to explore different approaches to priority based budgeting, while acknowledging that there is always going to be an imperfect and two-way relationship between strategies and budgets. The most likely outcome will be a mixture of incremental and priority based approaches.

- Councils wishing to move towards the construction of priority based budgets may wish to consider using decision support systems (such as decision conferencing), or may prefer to evolve their own approach (as shown in the examples of Sandwell MBC and Kirklees MBC).

10

Strategic management and organisational change

INTRODUCTION

In this final chapter, we discuss and illustrate the management challenge of introducing and sustaining a strategic approach to decision-making in a local authority. A strategic approach may include, but is certainly not confined to, the processes and products of strategic planning which have dominated the content of earlier chapters. In this chapter the *how* of strategic management is examined and planning, as opposed to the *what*. At the end of this chapter, we extract those elements of particular concern to practitioners.

The chapter deals with six discrete areas of strategic management:

- the main tasks of strategic management;
- the crucial role of 'strategic champions';
- implementation issues;
- organisational development – creating the right organisational climate;
- the dangers of over-formalisation;
- involving the public.

But first, as an over-riding theme of these areas of concern, it is important to re-emphasise a point made earlier in the Introduction, where we wrote:

> ... *what can be achieved in any one authority will depend crucially on its history and traditions, culture and current political and managerial climate. What might be an appropriate approach in one authority may be quite inappropriate in another. The political*

scope of what can be achieved will, in the short term at least, be much greater in some authorities than others. Ultimately the most appropriate way in which strategic choices should be identified, consolidated and managed will be unique to each authority.

It is important to reiterate this argument here, to guard against the danger of following the guidance set out below too literally. Indeed there are two further important implications of the above statement.

One of the most important skills of strategic management is the ability to understand both the opportunities and limitations of an authority's political and organisational culture and climate. If strategic planning involves an approach previously unfamiliar to the authority, then the way it is introduced will be critical. If such an approach is already established, then it is by no means uncommon for periodic re-examination or crises of confidence to be experienced. In either case a sensitive reading of culture and climate will lead to recommendations which will enable progress to be made (e.g. choices between comprehensive, topic-specific or service-based strategic approaches, *see* Chapter 3). Similarly, proposals which over-estimate the scope of opportunities, or which ignore or downplay the level of cultural 'resistance' are likely to struggle. It is beyond the scope of this book to specify in detail how such 'culture-reading skills' can be acquired. But we are well aware of their importance.

The second implication is that the managerial guidance set out in this text should be subjected to critical scrutiny by practitioner readers, in the light of their own knowledge of their authority and its particular characteristics. We are convinced of appropriateness of the principles set out below, and in the previous chapters. However, we readily acknowledge that the way in which they can and should be translated into action will vary from authority to authority. This view does not imply the sanctioning of a dismissive 'it's not appropriate here' response to strategic planning and management. We have already emphasised our conviction of their significance, even in authorities with a predominant 'service provision' role. But it is recognised that the scope for strategic approaches and the way they are introduced will be subject to considerable culturally influenced variety.

The tasks of strategic management

So far our discussion about strategic choices has centred on the role of strategic planning: the way in which such choices are collectively identified, explored, inter-related and then (usually) presented in documentary form, so that future corporate intentions and directions of the authority are made clear. Now it is appropriate to turn to strategic management, as opposed to strategic planning, and to identify the key tasks which this concept embraces. In our view, the term strategic management can imply either a range of activities which shape the process of strategic planning or which take forward its products into the realm of managerial action or both.

Much depends on the stage that the authority has already reached. If there is no tradition or recent experience of strategic planning, then the first set of tasks is as follows:

- encouraging the creation of an organisational climate in which the value of strategic planning will be recognised;

- judging when the time is right for the launch of a strategic initiative;

- assessing and advocating the most appropriate form of that strategic initiative in the light of the existing organisational climate and culture, and the future trajectory of these dimensions;

- nurturing the strategic initiative through the difficult early stages, when it is likely to experience criticism;

- developing the organisational capacity to sustain the strategic initiative and to demonstrate its viability.

If, on the other hand, there is already a well-established strategic planning process in operation, to which leading members or officers are committed, the tasks are rather different. Launching an initiative is not a problem; revitalising it, may be. In this situation they key tasks become:

- keeping the strategic process under review to ensure that it does not become stale, predictable, or routinised;

- ensuring that the organisational capacity exists to deliver on the strategy (what 'delivery' means in this context will be explained later);

- ensuring that organisational mechanisms exist to identify external changes and trends which may come to affect the strategic agenda;

- coping with unforeseen crises that may have a major impact on the authority.

Irrespective of whether an authority is unfamiliar with, or accustomed to, the idea of strategic planning, these last three tasks which can be labelled 'developing organisational capacity', 'environmental scanning' and 'crisis management' respectively are all crucial elements of strategic management.

Developing organisational capacity

As we have argued, all local authorities face a strategic agenda, which demands some form of response or choice. Even a local authority that has made no explicit commitment to strategic planning may be said to have a de facto strategic agenda which comprises what it has decided to do in relation to the set of external challenges facing it. For example, for a shire district, in 1993, this list could well have included the following:

■ whether to strive to win CCT contracts in-house, or not;

■ what to argue for when faced with the Local Government Review;

■ how to respond when a large local employer is threatened with closure;

■ how to respond (if at all) to Agenda 21;

■ whether or not to sell off existing council house stock to a specially established housing association and so realise a significant capital asset.

In so far as the authority's strategic agenda implies the need for cultural change, that too, in the first instance at least, is an important strategic management task. Publicly announcing a 'close to the customer' commitment is one thing. Ensuring that the organisation actually behaves in a way which reflects that value is another. That is why it is not in principle a waste of highly paid time for a chief executive to sit in at the locations where customers are received and responded to by council staff. Or if empowerment of local communities is made a key value, it may be a good use of senior management time to appear regularly in local community forums, assessing how best the value can be realised. The issue of building organisational capacity is returned to later in this chapter.

Environmental scanning

Equally important is the environmental scanning role. In essence this role involves the identification of changes or trends which may affect the current strategic agenda of the authority, or at least which imply the need for further strategic analysis. Some examples may help here. It is noticed that four or five shops in part of a town centre, previously regarded as prosperous, close and prove difficult to re-let. That small change could be a signal of underlying changes in the relative 'retail attractiveness' of different locations, which may require decisive remedial action (possibly a rethink of the town centre policy). Or let us say, there is a significant rise in the level of reported crime in a residential area that has previously been relatively crime-free. Or the rules for the allocation of lottery funds change, offering opportunities for one of the authority's priorities that did not previously exist. The potential importance of effective environmental scanning is an ability to identify potentially crucial changes while it is still possible to take pre-emptive action to limit the threat (or alternatively, early action to realise an opportunity). (*See also* Chapter 8.)

Crisis management

The third category of strategic management – crisis management – may involve a range of different types of crisis, some internal some external.

- A large local firm announces impending closure or expresses the intention to relocate.

- There is a serious child abuse incident, implying shortcomings in the operation of the social services department.

- Figures produced by a council DSO indicate the likelihood of failure for the second year in succession to reach a required rate of return.

- A prestigious theatre in the city centre reveals a financial crisis and announces that it will have to close next week, unless help is forthcoming.

As any chief executive will tell you, such incidents are unquestionably strategic, i.e. they have major implications for the council's public status, current priorities or demands on its budget and thus test to the limit the managerial capacity of senior managers. It is in such situations that the relationship of the leader/chief executive is put under the strongest pressure for such crises will certainly be of concern to the political parties, but the urgency with which a response is required may often require an initial decision by leader/chief executive.

The tasks of strategic management can usefully be summarised and depicted diagrammatically (*see* Fig. 10.1).

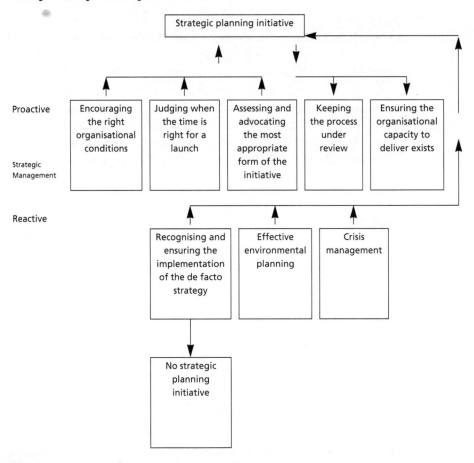

Fig. 10.1 The key tasks of strategic management

The crucial role of strategic champions

As we argued in Chapter 5, the development or continuation of a strategic initiative will always be subject to pressures for dilution or retraction, except in situations in which the strategy performs a predominantly symbolic function only in which case, of course, it is no real threat to anyone! That means that to succeed in changing the way decisions are made in a local authority a strategic initiative needs both organisational champions and appropriate organisational mechanisms to help establish it as a going concern.

The chief executive

The need for organisational champions arguably exists at three levels: chief executive; leading members; and middle management. It is unusual for a strategic launch not to be associated with a chief executive who is an enthusiastic champion of its benefits, although as we have seen an alternative model is that of an open-minded chief executive who is prepared to give a more committed deputy (or a member of a central planning unit) the authority and scope for action (*see* Chapter 6). What is likely to prove a major stumbling block, however, is a chief executive who is antipathetic to a strategic initiative, unless he or she has been marginalised by leading politicians.

> The need for strategic champions exists at three levels: chief executive; leading members; and middle management.

In principle, it can be argued that the job description of a chief executive should be dominated by 'strategic management'. Indeed, the main argument for a free-standing chief executive with no developmental responsibilities, supported by a small policy unit, is that strategic management is so important a task to the organisation that it requires a more or less full-time commitment from the person at the top. Strategic management will necessarily involve others also: the political leadership; members of the authority's management team; and the corporate policy unit (or its equivalent). But the lead role in strategic management (as opposed to strategic planning) should be the responsibility of the chief executive. It should be his or her job to structure and facilitate the way in which strategic choices are made. In this connection, let us highlight again the six primary types of strategic choice which face all lead authorities (see pp.17–18 above):

1. Choices to devote organisational time and energy to particular non-service specific objectives.

2. Choices between alternative means (or policies) for achieving a particular strategic objective.

3. Choices of priority between different strategic priorities when a conflict becomes apparent.

4. Choices as to which cultural attributes the organisation wishes to adopt and express.

5. Choices in response to an unanticipated crisis or external pressure for action.

6. Choices of initiative or change in organisational structure and processes in support of 1 to 4.

The first four type of choices are those which are best addressed within a strategic planning process, what should be politically led. The chief executive's task in this case is to judge how best to encourage, shape and facilitate the processes of choice involved. In the case of crisis/external pressures the task is to anticipate (as far as possible) such crises and pressures, to alert members to them and to ensure that they are responded to in the light of existing strategic direction. However, it is in relation to the sixth type of choice – choices of organisation structure, process or initiative to express or support strategic priorities – which are likely to take up most of the chief executive's time (see pp.130–4 below).

The role of policy units and secondments

Except perhaps in a small authority, the enthusiasm and commitment of a chief executive (or deputy) would not be enough to develop and sustain a number of key follow-up areas (developing links with the budget process, drawing up plans of action for each strategic objective and assessing the impact of such action) which are likely to prove crucial in demonstrating the value of the strategic initiative and for which a chief executive (or 'prime mover') needs to identify allies with a similar level of commitment. It may be possible to find individuals within the organisation who have the skills and commitment to carry out these tasks, and there are potential advantages in doing so, for such individuals are already likely to have access to networks of influence within the authority. If there exists a corporate planning (or policy planning) unit within the authority, that is one likely source of such skills/commitment. But within service departments there may be similar proclivities amongst town planners, for example, or indeed other professional areas where a planning role is emphasised, such as social services or economic development. Individuals within the finance department with a belief in the value of priority-based budgeting are a further important potential resource, particularly in situations where there is a more traditional treasurer in position, accustomed to incremental or bargaining methods of budgetary allocation.

The secondment of existing staff to development work on a strategic initiative is clearly easier to argue for in the current financial climate than is the appointment of new staff. If it does prove possible to identify existing staff with the requisite qualities the challenge then becomes one of negotiating their release from current responsibilities whether on a part-time or full-time basis. This task is likely to prove particularly difficult in authorities which have established 'business units', service level agreements or service-related performance targets for staff. In these circumstances 'secondment' appears in direct conflict with underlying business ethos of the authority. The resistance to such requests is of course a likely tactic on the part of chief officers who are suspicious about the implications of a strategic approach for their departmental autonomy and/or budget allocation.

In principle, a chief executive should be able to insist on secondment (if necessary 'buying in' the requisite time from his or her own budget). In practice, in an authority where the balance of power is still skewed towards service department/committees rather than the corporate centre, the negotiation process may be much more problematical.

Assuming that it has been possible to identify a team of strategic champions working to a chief executive (or lead officer) who is a strategic enthusiast, there remains (as discussed in Chapter 6) one further council area of championship – the elected members. Even if the first two conditions exist – support/enthusiasm at chief executive and middle management levels – a strategic initiative will fail unless there is generated a sufficient level of political commitment to sustain it.

Implementation issues

The link between strategy and implementation

There are various different ways of conceptualising, and of attempting to operationalise, the link between strategy and implementation. The *design approach* is deductive, and views implementation as the expression of strategy and as determined by the latter. The *learning approach* is inductive and views the strategy as an expression of discoveries and innovations made during implementation. These are the two main ways of conceiving of this relationship, and so Mintzberg (1994) suggests that the two can be combined by encouraging learning to occur within the strategic framework established by vision.

But a third possibility can also be suggested whereby existing or intended action programmes search around for strategies to support them, and mould themselves to the requirements of the latter, to give the appearance of being strategically determined. An example of this practice is the way in which local authorities identify activities they are planning to undertake in an area and shape these to the requirements of the Single Regeneration Budget so that they can be funded through this mechanism. This process (*strategic affinity*) may be regarded as cynical and opportunistic, but in so far as the actions concerned are consistent with the strategy, and are selected and carried forward because of these strategic links, then they are no less valid than activities which are strategically designed.

In practice we may well find a combination of learning, design and affinity, as demonstrated by the following example. An instance arose recently where a local authority was undertaking local area consultations on aspects of its planning policy. One of these consultations was attended by a leading member who was influential in a strategic context. This member saw the success of the area consultation exercise and, learning from this, suggested that area action plans should be adopted generally as a part of the council's corporate strategy, and implemented throughout the borough. Officers in other departments, however, were already undertaking their own local consultations, but were now in the position of being able to gain support for these by moulding them to the specifications of the corporate strategy. The three steps taken here, then, were learning, design and affinity.

Demonstrating results

It is important in sustaining the momentum of a strategic initiative that positive results are demonstrable over a relatively short time scale. In this connection, a successful SRB or lottery bid can have the desired effect. A positive public reaction can also be viewed as a success. But the expenditure of resources, even on a relatively small scale, may be needed to show that 'something is being done' (e.g. CCTV in a town centre to discourage crime). Whatever the long-term action or implications of a strategic priority, if successes can be demonstrated in the short term, members are more likely to sense the potential political spin-offs and increase their support for the strategic initiative.

Organisational development – creating the right climate

The two key management tasks already discussed – establishing a critical mass of strategic champions and (where appropriate) formalising their role into a new element of organisational structure; and identifying and operating effectively appropriate forums for strategy development and strategic management (*see* Chapter 6) can be seen as two examples of considerable importance in developing the organisational capacity to support strategic initiatives.

As Michael Clarke and John Stewart have rightly pointed out, strategic management does not 'just happen'. It needs an organisational base, and that organisational base needs protection within which strategic management as a process can develop and demonstrate 'added value'

> **Strategic management does not 'just happen'. It needs an organisational base within which strategic management as a process can develop.**

> *Strategic management runs counter to the normal way of working ... and it has a different perspective from the normal way of working – it sees what cannot be seen from the perspective of operational management. Strategic management enforces on 'organisational pause' – it provides a means of escape from the pressures of routine and the necessity of continuity (Clarke and Stewart 1991, p.61).*

Clarke and Stewart have argued that such an 'organisational pause' can only be achieved by protecting time and space for strategic management, pointing out that 'committees will never consider strategy if it is treated as another item on an agenda; and that officers who have dealt with strategy as another item in their in-tray of concern will never reach that item' (*ibid.*, p.61).

We have already noted the case for a small unit with the skills necessary for strategic management. Clarke and Stewart argue (1991, p.66) that this degree of formalisation is often helpful, and identifies the following necessary skills:

- skills in quantitative analysis;
- a capacity for qualitative analysis;
- organisational understanding;
- on appreciation of organisational development;
- political sensitivity and awareness.

They argue that such a unit 'must work with and through other parts of the organisation. Staff must be seconded to it. Working groups must support its work. Its role is to provide focus and give protection for the development of strategic management.'

A strategic approach and organisational development

The changes discussed above: establishment of an organisational pause; setting up of strategic forums; creation of a strategic planning unit are all important devices for kick-starting a strategy process within a local authority. But in the longer term, as we have already demonstrated, a strategic approach, if it is to be effective, must become part of the culture of the local authority and influence, where appropriate, the day-to-day actions of employees at all levels of the organisation. This is quite palpably true of the mission statement elements of corporate strategy. Statements of value about customer care, for example, are only meaningful in so far as they are internalised and applied by those who have contact with customers, or who plan customer services. But it is equally true of the priorities in a strategic vision statement. In the implementation of such priorities, staff other than the directors' board will necessarily play a key role. It is important that they should understand the meaning and significance of the strategy, and what it implies for their behaviour, above and beyond any specific implementation responsibilities they may have. As we have argued the adoption of a strategic approach is a statement of a new perspective in relation to organisational role and behaviour. It will thus necessarily have important organisational development implications. These implications may be summarised under three headings:

- encouraging a bottom-up as well as a top-down approach to strategy;

- making the organisational values come to life;

- enhancing a corporate perspective to problem solving.

Bottom up as well as top-down

Co-ordination and the breaking down of departmental barriers, leading to the emergence of corporate priorities, can be stimulated from two different directions. First of all they can be initiated from the centre of the organisation through the activities of the political leadership (chief executive or chief officers) in reaction to divisions and rivalries between departments. This process was discussed in Chapter 5.

But corporate priorities can also be stimulated by contact with the public and the recipients of council services, who are ignorant of departmental boundaries and are simply concerned to get a service which meets their requirements in the simplest and most direct way. The point to emphasise in the context of organisation development is the way in which this 'bottom-up' approach depends upon those working at or behind the front line for insights as to service co-ordination problems, or public concerns which overlap or fall between defined areas of service responsibility. Such insights will be encouraged by assurances from above that they will be welcomed and taken seriously. In training and development terms the inclusion of front line staff in strategy task forces designed to provide solutions to the co-ordination problems identified is to be commended.

Breathing life into organisational value

In discussing the way in which organisational values can be transformed from worthy statements in council publicity material to a source of real behavioural change, the concept of 'testability' was emphasised. The issue is how an authority which supports these values should differ from one which does not do so, not merely in day-to-day working, but in dealing with difficult issues.

The point is, that for an authority serious about translating core values into cultural reality, the case for both effective education programmes and the development and application of value-indicators becomes transparent; otherwise the core values are likely to remain as symbolic devices. The circulation of explanatory memoranda is unlikely to change habits. A serious commitment to consultation with staff over the meaning of core values, appropriate training to develop the new understandings and skills required, and regular review sessions are all essential requirements.

Enhancing a corporate perspective

There is of course, more to a corporate strategy than corporate values, important though these are. The substantive corporate agenda of an authority also has organisational development implications. As we discussed in Chapter 5, the origins of a strategic approach are usually centred around the chief executive and council leader. But if corporate objectives are to make a real impact upon an authority's actions and generate the commitment of time and financial resources from departments, they need a much wider commitment amongst senior staff than this. There is, as we implied in Chapter 5, an initial task of gaining the commitment of other members of the management team (or directors' board) so that they do not obstruct the development and application of the strategy, particularly at budget time. But equally important is the commitment of middle managers. If an authority can establish a critical mass of middle managers who understand the need for a corporate strategy and who recognise a responsibility to 'act corporately' as well as managerially, in relation to their departmental responsibilities, then the authority can indeed claim to have 'changed its culture'. Again there is a training implication; the investment of resources in either internal or external training courses which focus on strategic planning and management at the corporate level.

As Clarke and Stewart have pointed out, 'organisational development is the key instrument of strategic management'. In addition to the measures discussed in more detail above, strategic organisational development may also involve:

- an understanding of organisational strengths and weaknesses;

- a capacity to analyse strategic change into organisational needs;

- skills in organisational design, and the avoidance of over-design;

- positive communication skills: listening as well as telling;

- space for staff involvement in organisational change;

- training policies grounded in the plans for organisational development;

- developmental opportunities for staff related to the organisational changes sought;

- recruitment and promotion policies geared to organisational change.

Strategic management is not an easy concept to grasp and exemplify. We have tried to characterise it in terms of what it should do. There is value, however, in approaching the issue from a different perspective, and illustrating the nature of strategic management by identifying what it should not do. In this connection, Clarke and Stewart's 'twelve common mistakes in strategic management' involve an invaluable source of insight (Clarke and Stewart 1991, pp.71–4).

Twelve common mistakes in strategic management

1. *To reduce strategic management to a routine*
   If strategic management becomes a routine set of procedures to be carried out each year, it becomes so much a part of the normal way of working that it loses its capacity to add value. Strategic management must have a different rhythm from the normal way of working. It is developed in an organisational pause not in the rhythm of organisational continuity.

2. *To mistake a strategic plan for strategic management*
   A strategic plan may be a useful instrument in strategic management, recording the need for a change and communicating a sense of direction, but it is not itself strategic management. Strategic management is about organisational change. It takes place not in a plan, but in change itself.

3. *To assume a set of objectives itself provides an adequate basis for a strategy for change*
   A set of objectives may be useful in the management of the authority in showing direction, but a set of objectives is not by itself a basis for a strategy. The real issues for organisational change lie not in objectives but in the inter-relationships between them. Strategic management cannot take objectives as setting a strategy. Strategy lies in the balance between objectives.

4. *To confuse strategic management with planning and programming*
   A local authority may need objectives, performance requirements, programmes of action, management targets and performance review. These should be part of its normal way of working. These are basic management requirements. However, these requirements should not be mistaken for strategic management, although strategic management may use these for organisational change as it will use other organisational instruments. Strategic management is defined by its own distinctive contribution.

5. *To ignore organisational development*
   This is the commonest, but also the most fundamental mistake. It assumes that strategic change, i.e. change in activities or way of working, can be carried out by an organisation that has up to now failed to make the change. A strategy unrelated to organisation development will be frustrated by organisational inertia.

6. *To assume a vision is possible*
   A vision assumes an end state, when a local authority has achieved its objectives. But a local authority can never achieve its objectives, because the world does not stand still. Objectives change with a changing world. Strategic management is not about achieving a vision, but about learning, adapting and developing.

7. *To presume certainty*
   A strategy or a set of objectives can appear to impose certainty, but there can be no certainty in local government. Needs change, aspirations grow, the political process challenges, opportunities arise. Strategic management is about coping with uncertainty – learning, adapting and developing.

8. *To seek the comprehensive approach*
   If strategic management covers everything it has failed to identify the strategic. Selectivity is at the heart of strategic management – the identification of the key changes, which the existing organisation is incapable of undertaking.

9. *Not realising that strategic management must let go*
   Issues will become the concern of strategic management. They should not remain its concern. It is the task of strategic management to work out what is required, and to effect the organisational changes needed. If strategic management is still required to be involved, it has failed because it has not built an organisational capacity that can itself resolve the issue.

10. *To limit resource consideration to financial issues*
    Strategic management should involve strengthening organisational capacity and realising organisational potential. That involves the full use of all the resources of the authority staff, information, powers, property and equipment. Strategic management is not merely about the full use of those resources, but also about their development.

11. *To restrict strategic management to the organisational boundaries*
    Operational management focuses on the activities of the authority. It is necessarily restricted to the boundaries set by those activities. Strategic management can look beyond those boundaries to problems not faced and to community resources not realised.

12. *To restrict strategic management to a strategic unit*
    Strategic management requires protection in the working of the authority. That may require the creation of a special unit to provide a focus for strategic management. The danger is to mistake a necessary focus for the whole of strategic management. Strategic management isolated in a unit may produce a strategy but will not change any organisation or influence action.

The dangers of over-formalisation

One of the characteristic features of a business plan is the specification of measurable 'targets' which are subsequently used as indicators of business success. Some illustrations are listed below:

■ a target of reducing the average proportion of unoccupied council houses to two per cent;

■ a target of achieving one per cent above the required minimum rate of return for a DSO;

■ a target of reaching decisions on 95 per cent of all planning applications within 6 weeks of receipt;

■ an income target for housing benefit fraud recovery which covers the costs of the unit concerned.

In principle, assessment of success in responding to strategic issues or achieving strategic objectives is equally desirable. However, there is also a real danger of too hasty or comprehensive an attempt to judge a strategy in terms of success or otherwise in meeting measurable targets.

This danger stems from the fact that most strategic issues are different from most service-specific issues. John Stewart (1995a, p.40) has coined the term 'wicked issues' to characterise problems of great complexity and resilience to solution such as crime (and the associated fear of crime), traffic congestion in towns and cities, and the challenge of economic regeneration in an area which has lost its basic industry.

Wicked issues are examples of particularly challenging strategic priorities. It is of course possible to set targets for such priorities – reducing crime levels by a certain percentage, reducing journey times to a city centre, decreasing levels of unemployment – but to do so at too early a stage often unhelpfully oversimplifies the problem.

For wicked issues there are no easy answers, if there were it would not be justifiable to define them as 'strategic'. For such issues there is a high premium on 'policy learning'. Action will often of necessity be explorative and experimental rather than definitive. Controlled pilot schemes, new initiatives in which there are unavoidable elements of 'trial and error', opportunities for joint action with other agencies which may or may not prove beneficial – all these provide examples of the kind of measures appropriate in the early stages of responding to a strategic issue. Solutions to the underlying problems involved are likely to be achievable only in the longer term, indeed in some cases a worsening of the problem may be anticipated before things get better, particularly if unforeseen changes or crises occur which accentuate the problem.

In these circumstances the identification of targets of achievement may feel more like millstones than incentives! Certainly there is a symbolic value in demonstrating some early success (e.g. the impact of CCTV on crime in town centres), but that apart, strategic issues have to be explored and experimented upon and targets can hinder rather than facilitate this process. Targets are in any event more problematic in application when the local authority does not have the sole responsibility for the implementation of the measures concerned. There may come a time when it is helpful to specify targets but only when a level of understanding of the problems has been reached and a momentum of activity has been built up.

Over-zealous target-setting for strategic priorities is one danger. The second is their incorporation into policy planning systems. Policy planning systems typically involve regular annual updates of a series of policy parameters – demographic, financial, legislative – which may be expecting to influence the need for particular forms of council activity. Normally policy planning systems are used in conjunction with the budget process, in which they are used to demonstrate the changing demand for school places vis-à-vis services for fragile elderly, for example, in line with demographic trends.

Clearly there is value in this kind of activity. In Chapter 9 we set out in some detail an example of budget-related policy planning system in Sandwell MBC which has proved a major improvement of previous practice. However, if an attempt is made to incorporate strategic priorities of a non-service-specific nature into policy planning system it runs the risk of trying to treat two different types of issue as though they were similar. As we have argued, strategic planning is not an alternative to service planning, it is something which provides added value. Secondly, as we showed in relation to 'performance indicators' strategic issues tend to be more intractable with action necessarily more tentative than would be the case for an established service area. The incorporation of strategic objectives into a policy planning system blurs that important distinction. Indeed, the political impetus of a strategic agenda may be lost if that agenda became submerged in what may appear to be a bewildering technocratic and sometimes mechanistic approach. There may of course be ways in which a strategic agenda can be reflected in a policy planning system – a commitment, for example, to a particular age-group or a determination to protect a particular service would certainly have repercussions. The mistake is to treat the entire strategic agenda in this way.

Strategic planning can be viewed as a delicate and tender plant, which requires time, space and careful attention to develop and prosper. Premature formalisation as illustrated by the two examples discussed above is one of the main potential threats to its growth.

Public involvement in strategic planning

It was argued in Chapter 2 that one of the potential benefits of corporate strategy is its capacity to generate public interest and involvement, at a time when local government needs all the public interest and involvement it can get. It is appropriate, therefore, to look at the experience of those authorities which have consulted the public on the contents of strategic plans.

One of the early success stories, in this respect was the initiative taken by the London Borough of Sutton, who have from 1991 onwards put out their draft statement of strategic priorities for public consultation and made amendments in the light of that consultation. Figure 10.2 provides an illustration from Wyre District Council of an attempt to present strategic priorities and choices in a form which is accessible to the general public.

A number of lessons can be learned about how best to involve the public in strategy formulation, although it must be emphasised that these lessons are based on a relatively small number of examples:

- It should be made clear, that the strategy is a draft or 'first shot', and that the authority is prepared to modify it in the light of public opinion. If it is regarded as a 'fait accompli' (or if that characteristic becomes clear in the lack of changes subsequently made) then it is likely to increase public cynicism rather than commitment or interest.

- The strategy should present real choices, so that the public do not end up merely acquiescing with a number of worthy long-term desiderata.

- The version of strategy which is presented to public must be user-friendly – attractively laid out, well illustrated, and eye-catching – which will in most cases imply a different version to that used for internal discussion (although the content must, of course, be consistent).

- When a corporate strategy is finally adopted by the council, it should be made clear how public response has been taken on board both where it has resulted in changes, and (equally important) the reasons for not taking on board other changes for which there was significant public support.

Conclusion

Strategic management, as we saw in Chapter 1, involves the capacity to identify and respond to significant choices – i.e. choices with major implications for future success, effectiveness, well-being or identity. As a process it is applicable in principle to individuals, small working groups, sections, departments and organisations as corporate entities. In this book we have concentrated on the organisation as a corporate entity, and shown how processes of strategic planning and management can indeed contribute to organisational identity, effectiveness and well-being. We have argued that these processes must 'add value' to the more familiar processes of operational management within an authority. We have suggested that to do this, strategic initiatives must be selective, focusing on the 'big issues' and not intruding upon aspects of organisational operations where they are inappropriate. In relation to core values, it is true that, to be effective, a strategy is likely to have implications for the behaviour of all staff members (consider, for example, the implications of the value of 'good communication', 'customer responsiveness or 'equal opportunities'). However, many aspects of staff behaviour will be untouched by corporate strategic priorities – and rightly so.

Wyre Borough Council

Community Plan 1996–97

Wyre Borough Council is committed to meeting its Vision, which is:

"To work with all sections of the community to secure top quality services, promote a successful economy, represent local interests, and maintain a safe, healthy and attractive environment".

In order that you can see what the Council intends to do, we have produced this Community Plan. It shows the main things that the Council has set itself to do in 1996-97. At the end of the year (ie in April 1997) we will publish what we have done in relation to these objectives so that you can see for yourself how far we have met them.

All these objectives are over and above the normal services of the Council. We will continue to deliver those services to a high standard. We will also try to improve them throughout the year. You can help us in this by giving us your views about how well we do and about different ways we could do things. Any views are welcome.

The Community Plan is a new idea. We hope you find it useful in finding out how well your Council serves you.

Richard Anyon
Leader of the Council

Planning

PL1. Make a decision on at least 80% of householder planning applications within eight weeks of receiving them.

PL2. Make a decision on at least 60% of other planning applications within eight weeks of receiving them.

PL3. Win at least 65% of planning appeals.

PL4. Make a successful submission for the Charter Mark for planning application and appeal services.

PL5. Establish a system for assessing customer

opinions of planning application and appeal services, as part of the Charter Mark submission.

PL6. Hold a Public Inquiry for the Council's Borough-wide Local Plan.

Traffic and Transport

TT1. Actively lobby for improvements to the transport infrastructure serving the Borough.

TT2. Introduce new management measures for the control of off-street car parking within the Borough and the improvement of car parks.

TT3. Investigate possible new ways of controlling on-street parking in selected areas of the Borough.

TT4. Develop, adopt and implement (where possible) comprehensive plans for the centres of Poulton-le-Fylde, Cleveleys and Fleetwood, reviewing pedestrianisation, traffic management and transport coordination.

TT5. Review and update the Council's Road Safety Strategy.

TT6. Commence a review of all Traffic Regulation Orders.

Environmental Services

ES1. Develop shoreline management plans which will provide for continuing effective defence against the sea.

ES2. Implement the Council's Environmental Improvements programme including "Pride of Place" schemes.

ES3. Assist in carrying out other environmental improvement schemes wherever funds are available.

ES4. Develop the medium term objectives of the recycling plan by recycling 12% of domestic waste by the end of the year and by writing a strategy for the long term.

ES5. Explore ways of further improving the refuse collection service.

ES6. Develop, alone or with other Districts in Lancashire, an Air Quality Monitoring system to meet the requirements of the Environment Act 1995.

ES7. Take action to minimise the financial effect on the Council of the national Landfill Tax, particularly by devising and implementing a system of sustainable waste management.

Countryside and Tourism

CT1. Launch a Borough-wide Countryside Management Strategy .

CT2. Carry out a programme of schemes to enhance conservation, recreation and access in both the wider countryside and in the green spaces close to where people live and work.

CT3. Encourage and assist the involvement and participation of local communities in the conservation and enhancement of the countryside.

CT4. Assist appropriate Countryside and Tourism organisations in their applications for funds from the National Lottery and other grant-aiding bodies.

CT5. Launch a new Borough-wide strategy for Tourism.

CT6. Work with public, private and voluntary sector partners to implement the proposals of the Tourism Strategy.

CT7. Make Tourist Information Centres increasingly attractive and useful to residents.

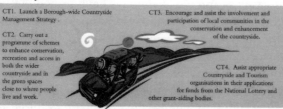

Fig. 10.2 Wyre Borough Council's community plan

Sport and Leisure

SL1. Develop a strategy for sport and leisure.

SL2. Undertake an audit of the Arts within the Borough.

SL3. Review the Council's concessions for the use of Sports and Leisure facilities.

SL4. Assist appropriate leisure organisations in their applications to obtain funds from the National Lottery.

SL5. Effectively retender and implement the Council's Grounds Maintenance contracts.

SL6. Effectively retender and implement the Council's Indoor and Outdoor Recreation contracts.

SL7. Introduce a regular appropriate market at Marsh Mill-in-Wyre.

SL8. Develop and implement anti-vandalism patrols in parks, cemeteries and open spaces throughout the Borough.

Business Services

BS1. Make the Council's services to local businesses more accountable, more business like, more open and more tailored to customers' needs.

BS2. Forge closer working partnerships with businesses, placing advice and guidance ahead of enforcement.

BS3. Review the Council's links with education establishments and its contribution to industry/education links throughout the Borough.

BS4. Resolve the long-term arrangements for management and land use of Jameson Road landfill site.

BS5. Hold successful Business Advice events.

BS6. Implement the Council's policy on trading patterns at Fleetwood market.

Economic Development

ED1. Set up and play an active part in the Fleetwood Regeneration Partnership.

ED2. Assist the Fleetwood Regeneration Partnership to make a successful bid for money for Fleetwood from the Single Regeneration Budget.

ED3. Make a successful bid for funds from the European Union PESCA Community Initiative.

ED4. Devise and submit suitable projects for other European Union funds including Objective 5b (for the designated part of the rural area) and the Ouverture Pilot Initiative (for tourism in rural areas).

ED5. Assist ICI to market the Hillhouse International site as a location for new job-creating investment.

ED6. Assist in the regeneration of the Fleetwood Dockland and Marsh areas.

ED7. Assist in the relocation and expansion of Wyre Community Services.

ED8. Play a full part in the successful establishment and operation of the Fylde Coast Business Link.

ED9. Promote actively the potential of Fleetwood as a fishing port through the Fleetwood Fish Forum.

ED10. Produce a single database of current economic information on Wyre in support of applications for funds.

General Services To Customers

CS1. Ensure that, for all telephone calls received on the main switchboard at least 70% are answered within ten seconds and at least 90% within twenty seconds.

CS2. Ensure that all letters requiring a reply receive within ten working days either a full response or an acknowledgement indicating when a full response and/or action is likely.

CS3. Review the Council's policy on, and criteria for, making grants to Local Organisations and review its application procedures accordingly.

CS4. Investigate the value and viability of a "first-stop-shop" at each of the Council's publicly accessible offices.

CS5. Present the Council's published documents in clear and simple language and format.

CS6. Make significant progress towards the award of Investor in People.

CS7. Ensure that all the Council's buildings open to the public are readily accessible to disabled persons.

CS8. Make a successful application for the Charter Mark for the Council's Revenue services.

Housing

HO1. Work closely with Wyre Housing Association to make a successful start on the provision of 200 new dwellings.

HO2. Work closely with Wyre Housing Association to ensure that the homeless and nominations responsibilities of the Council are properly discharged.

HO3. Review the provision of temporary accommodation at Norcross House.

HO4. Investigate the merits of establishing a Housing Advice Centre in Fleetwood.

HO5. Support the regeneration of private sector housing in Pharos Ward by targeting grants, encouraging Housing Associations to rehabilitate Houses in Multiple Occupation, and investigating the establishment of a renewal area.

HO6. Develop an "Empty Homes Strategy" for the Borough.

HO7. Work with private landlords to improve energy efficiency and safety measures in Houses in Multiple Occupation.

HO8. Undertake a private housing stock condition survey throughout the Borough.

HO9. Work with Housing Associations and private sector companies to develop innovative schemes to alleviate housing need throughout the Borough.

Strategic management is best seen as a way of thinking and working which is appropriate to some situations but not to others. As a process it is likely to dominate the working life of the chief executive, or at least should do so. For a receptionist in an area office, it will be a much smaller component of his or her working life – but still relevant. For example, a receptionist's impressionistic view of those attending the office (and the problems they present) may be of considerable strategic significance to the authority. In this sense, strategic management is really about organisational learning, not just at its apex but in and through the perceptions of its grass roots staff. Thus the ideal is a local authority in which the value of, and capacity for, learning is cherished at all levels – authority-wide, departmental, sectional and individual. As Clarke and Stewart (1991, p.23) have rightly argued:

> *A process of strategic management is about changing the organisation in relation to the strategic choices made . . . doing this requires a learning model. Above all it is appropriate to local government, if local government is seen as the means by which community choice and community voice is expressed. Local government becomes the means of community learning. The process of strategic management should determine all other planning process.*

SUMMARY

- In an authority with little previous experience of strategic initiatives, the key tasks of strategic management are as follows:

    (i)   encouraging the creation of an organisational climate in which the value of strategic planning will be recognised;

    (ii) judging when the time is right for the launch of a strategic initiative;

    (iii) assessing and advocating the most appropriate form of that strategic initiative in the light of the existing organisational climate and culture, and the future trajectory of these dimensions;

    (iv) nurturing the strategic initiative through the difficult early stages, when it is likely to experience criticism;

    (v)   developing the organisational capacity to sustain the strategic initiative and to demonstrate its viability.

- In authorities where there is already a well-established strategic and learning process, the key role of strategic management is:

    (i)   keeping the strategic process under review to ensure that it does not become stale, predictable, or routinised;

    (ii) ensuring that the organisational capacity exists to deliver on the strategy (what 'delivery' means in this context will be explained later);

    (iii) ensuring that organisational mechanisms exist to identify external changes and trends which may come to affect the strategic agenda;

    (iv) coping with unforeseen crises that have a major impact on the authority.

- The time and job description of a chief executive should be dominated by strategic management tasks, as illustrated by the above lists.

- The secondment of existing staff to development work on a strategic initiative is clearly easier to argue for in the current financial climate than is the appointment of new staff. If it does prove possible to identify existing staff with the requisite qualities the challenge then becomes one of negotiating their release from current responsibilities whether on a part-time or full-time basis.

- The strategy, in whatever form it is established, must be able to demonstrate at a relatively early stage of implementation a tangible impact on the problems identified.

- There are different ways in which the link between strategy and implementation can be analysed: the design, learning, and affinity of approaches. The design approach views implementation as the expression of strategy determined by it; the learning approach views strategy as an expression of discourse and innovations made during implementation; the affinity approach involves the repackaging of activities the authority was planning to undertake anyway.

- Strategic management does not 'just happen'. It needs an organisational base, and that organisational base needs protection within which strategic management as a process can develop and demonstrate 'added value'. It requires an 'organisational pause'.

- There is a case for the establishment of a small policy unit to support strategic management processes. Such a unit must work with and through other parts of the organisation. Staff must be seconded to it. Working groups must support its work. Its role is to provide focus and give protection for the development of strategic management.

- The key requisite skills of a policy unit include:

    (i) skills in quantitative analysis;

    (ii) a capacity for qualitative analysis;

(iii) organisational understanding;

(iv) an appreciation of organisational development;

(v) political sensitivity and awareness.

- Strategic management has important organisational development implications in particular:

    (i) encouraging a bottom-up as well as top down approach to strategy, by encouraging front-line staff to identify co-ordination and implementation gap problems;

    (ii) training on the behavioural implications of organisational values, to make the values come to life;

    (iii) training to build up a critical mass of staff with a corporate approach to management and problem solving.

- In the early stage of a strategic initiative, the identification of targets may feel more like millstones than incentives. There may come a time when it is helpful to specify targets but only when a level of understanding of the problems has been reached and a momentum of activity has been built up.

- If an attempt is made to incorporate strategic priorities of a non-service-specific nature into policy planning systems it runs the risk of trying to treat different types of issues as though they were similar. Indeed, the political impetus of a strategic agenda may be lost if that agenda became submerged in what may appear to be bewildering technocratic and sometimes mechanistic approach.

- There are a number of potential benefits in consulting the public in relation to a corporate strategy. The following points should, however, be borne in mind.

    (i) It should be clear, that the strategy is a draft or 'first shot', and that the authority is prepared to modify it in the light of public opinion. If it is regarded as a 'fait accompli' then it is likely to increase public cynicism rather than commitment or interest.

    (ii) The strategy should then present real choices, so that the public do not end up merely acquiescing with a number of worthy long-term desiderata.

    (iii) The version of strategy which is presented to the public must be user-friendly – attractively laid out, well illustrated and eye-catching which will in most cases imply a differently styled version to that used for internal discussion.

- Strategic management processes must 'add value' to the more familiar processes of operational management within an authority. To do this, strategic initiatives must be selective, focusing on the 'big issues' and not intruding upon aspects of organisational operations where they are inappropriate.

- A process of strategic management is about changing the organisation in relation to the strategic choices made ... doing this requires a learning model. Above all it is appropriate to local government, if local government is seen as the means by which community choice and community voice is expressed. Local government becomes the means of community learning that the process of strategic management should determine all other planning processes.

References

Ansoff, H.I. (1965) *Corporate Strategy: an Analytical Approach to Business Policy for Growth and Expansion*, McGraw Hill.

Audit Commission (1988) *The Competitive Council*, HMSO.

Audit Commission (1989) *More Equal Than Others: the Chief Executive in Local Government*, HMSO.

Audit Commission (1996) *We Can't Go On Meeting Like This*, HMSO.

Benington, J. (1976) *Local Government Becomes Big Business*, Community Development Project Research and Intelligence Unit, London.

Benson, J.K. (1975) 'The inter-organisational network as a political economy' *Administrative Science Quarterly*, Vol. 20, No. 2 (July).

Caulfield, I. and Schultz, J. (1989) *Planning for Change: Strategic Planning in Local Government*, Longman.

Chartered Institute of Public Finance and Accountancy (1990) *Financial Skills for Service Managers*, CIPFA.

Clarke, M. and Stewart, J. (1988) *The Enabling Council*, Local Government Training Board, Luton.

Clarke, M. and Stewart, J. (1990) *General Management in Local Government: Getting the Balance Right*, Longman.

Clarke, M. and Stewart, J. (1991) *Strategies for Success*, Local Government Management Board, Luton.

Cockburn, C. (1977) *The Local State*, Pluto Press.

Collinge, C. (1996) 'The limits of strategy', *Local Government Studies*, Autumn, Vol. 22, No. 4, pp.273–280.

Collinge, C. (1997) 'Political power and corporate managerialism in local government: the organisation of executive functions', *Environment and Planning C: Government and Policy*, Vol. 15, pp.347–361.

Collinge, C. and Leach, S. (1995) 'Building the capacity for strategy formation in local government' *Local Government Studies*, Autumn, Vol. 21, No. 3, pp.343–352.

Collinge, C. and Leach, S. (1995) 'New approaches to budget setting: a research agenda', in *Public Finance Foundation Review*, No. 8, November, pp.6–10.

Crozier, M. (1964) *The Bureaucratic Phenomenon*, Tavistock Publications.

Cyert, R.M. and March, J.G. (1963) *A Behavioural Theory of the Firm*, Prentice Hall.

DoE (1993) *Community Leadership and Representation: Unlocking the Potential*, HMSO.

References

Dunleavy, P. (1991) *Democracy, Bureaucracy and Public Choice*, Harvester Wheatsheaf.

Elcock, H. and Jordon, A. (eds) (1987) *Learning from Local Authority Budgeting*, Avebury Press.

Elcock, H., Jordan, A. and Midwinter, A. (1989) *Budgeting in Local Government: Managing the Margins*, Longman.

Epsom and Ewell DC (1996) *Corporate Strategy*.

Finer, H. (1950) *English Local Government*, (4th edn), Methuen.

Friend, J.K. and Jessop, W.N. (1969) *Local Government and Strategic Choice: An Operational Research Approach to the Process of Public Planning*, Tavistock Publications.

Greenwood, R. (1983) 'Changing patterns and budgeting in English local government', *Public Administration*, Vol. 61, No. 2, pp.149–168.

Greenwood, R. (1987) 'Managerial strategies in local government', *Public Administration*, Vol. 65, No. 3, pp.295–312.

Hyman, R. (1972) *Strikes*, Fontana.

Johnson, J. and Scholes, K. (1984) *Explorations in Corporate Strategy*, Prentice Hall International.

Keith-Lucas, B. and Richards, P.G. (1978) *A History of Local Government in the Twentieth Century*, Allen and Unwin.

Kotter, J. and Lawrence, P. (1974) *Mayors in Action: Five Approaches to Urban Governance*, Wiley.

Labour Party (1995) *Renewing Communities*, Labour Party.

Leach, S., Stewart, J. and Walsh, K. (1994) *The Changing Organisation and Management of Local Government*, Macmillan.

Leach, S., Walsh, K., Game, G., Rogers, S., Skelcher, C. and Spencer, K. (1993) *Challenge of Change: Characteristics of Good Management in Local Government*, Local Government Management Board.

Leach, S. and Hall, D. (1996) *Changing Forms of Local Politics*, Final Report to ESRC.

Leach, S. and Hall, S. (1997) *Social and Economic Trends*, Local Government Management Board, Luton.

Leicestershire City Council (1987) *Strategic Steering in Hung Authorities*, (Mimeo).

Lindblom, C. (1959) 'The science of muddling through', *Public Administration Review*, Vol. 29, No. 6.

Local Government Management Board (1994) *Fitness for Purpose: Shaping New Patterns of Organisation and Management*, LGMB, Luton.

Local Government Management Board (1997) *Social and Economic Trends*, LGMB, Luton.

Maud, J. (1966) 'Society of Town Clerks' Conference', *Municipal Review*, September, p.495.

Midwinter, A. and McGarvey, N. (1995) 'Organising the new Scottish Local Authorities – some problems with the new management agenda', *Local Government Policy-Making*, Vol. 22, No. 1 (July).

Mintzberg, H. (1991) *The Strategy Process: Concepts, Contexts, Cases*, Prentice Hall International.

Mintzberg, H. (1994) *The Rise and Fall of Strategic Planning*, Prentice Hall International.

Niskanen, W. (1971) *Bureaucracy and Representative Government*, Aldine Atherton.

Noble, J. and Collinge, C.J. (1993) 'Budget making through priorities', *Local Government Chronicle*, 12 February.

Osborne, D. and Gaebler, T. (1992) *Reinventing Government: How the Entrepreneurial Spirit is Transforming the Public Sector: From Schoolhouse to Statehouse, City Hall to Pentagon*, Addison-Wesley.

Peters, T.J. and Waterman, R.H. (1982) *In Search of Excellence: Lessons from America's Best Run Companies*, Harper Row.

Pinch, P.L. (1995) 'Governing urban finance: changing budgetary strategies in British local government', *Environment and Planning A*, Vol. 27, pp.965–983.

Redlich, J. and Hirst, F.W. (1970) *The History of Local Government in England*, Macmillan.

Roberts, G. and Scholes, K. (1993) 'Policy and base budget reviews at Cheshire County Council: making zero-based budgeting work', in *Proceedings of the Waves of Change Conference*, Sheffield.

Simon, H.A. (1957) *Administrative Behaviour: A Study of Decision Making Processes in Administration*, Macmillan.

Skelcher, C. (1992) *Managing for Service Quality*, Longman.

Smellie, K.B. (1968) *A History of Local Government*, Allen and Unwin.

Sotarauta, M. (1995) 'Governance of change by soft strategy: in search of new approaches for governing community development', working paper.

Stewart, J. (1995a) *Local Government Today: an Observer's View*, Local Government Management Board, Luton.

Stewart, J. (1995b) *Testing Organisational Values* (Mimeo), Institute of Local Government Studies, Birmingham.

Stewart, J. (1996) 'A dogma of our times: the separation of policy-making and implementation', *Public Money and Management*, July–September.

Thompson, G., Frances, J., Levačić, R., Mitchell, J. (eds) (1991) *Markets, Hierarchies and Networks: the Co-ordination of Social Life*, Sage.

Waller, P. (1983), *Town, City and Nation: England 1850–1914*, Oxford University Press.

Wheare, K.C. (1955) *Government by Committee: an Essay on the British Constitution*, Oxford University Press.

References

Wildavsky, A. (1973) 'If planning is everything maybe it's nothing', *Policy Sciences*, Vol. 4, pp.127–153.

Wildavsky, A. (1975) *Budgeting*, Little Brown.

Wildavsky, A. (1979) *Politics of the Budgetary Process*, (3rd edn), Little Brown.

Wraith, R.E. (1966) 'Institutional training for local government', *Municipal Review*, March, p.132.

Young, K. and Mills, L. (1993, 1997) *Survey of Internal Organisational Change in Local Government: the Corporate Survey*, Local Government Management Board, London.

Index

Agenda 21 91, 124
anti-poverty strategies 36, 56, 64
asset management 64
Audit Commission 36, 68

Bains Committee Report (1972) 9, 31, 34
Barnsley MBC 64–5
base budget review 110
Basildon DC 72
Bexley LBC 89–90
Birmingham City Council 20, 113
Braintree DC 72
Brent LBC 20, 56
Brighton City Council 75
Bristol City Council 74
budget processes (and strategy) xii, 105–20
'bureau shaping' 44, 50
business plans 22

Calderdale MBC 73, 75
Caulfield, Ian x
Chamberlain, Joseph 30
Chelmsford BC 89
Cheltenham BC 92
chief executives (in local government) 31–2, 54, 55–6, 67, 68, 87, 125, 127
  relationship with leaders 58–60
citizenship 77, 78
City Challenge 106, 108
client–contractor relations 11, 43
closed circuit television CCTV 130, 137
commercialism (in local government) 20, 56

communication 75, 78
community 13, 74, 77, 78
Community Care Plans 22
community governance 6, 12, 16, 20, 77, 101
community health 92
community plans 52
community safety (crime prevention) 10, 47, 91, 137
comprehensive approaches (to strategic planning) 25
compulsory competitive tendering (CCT) 5, 6, 124
Conservative party 56, 57, 105
contracting out (of council services) 36
core values ix, 1, 24, 26, 71–85
corporate planning and management 9, 18, 29–32, 35–6, 43
corporate strategy 14–15, 19, 23, 31, 35–40, 45–8, 56
council tax capping 6, 46
crisis management 125
Crosland Authority 10
customer care 74, 77, 78, 124

decision conferencing 114–15
departmentalism 30, 31, 42–4, 88
Direct Service Organisations (DSOs) xii
'direct service provision' 20, 45
Dudley MBC 91, 113

Ealing LBC 72, 91
East Hants DC 91

economic development regeneration
role 10, 24, 36, 47, 91, 137
Education Act 1988 42
elected mayors (USA) 30
electoral turn-out 14
empowerment 96–7
enabling role 16, 68
environmental sustainability 10, 24,
47, 91, 95
Epsom and Ewell DC 98–101
equality 75, 78, 79, 115
European Structure Funding 108
European Union (EU) 108

forums (for strategy) 60–5, 69–71
fragmentation (of local government)
15, 16, 33, 58

games (and strategy) 4–5
Grant-Maintained Status (GMS) 89
Great Yarmouth BC 75

Harman, John 119
Harrow LBC 72
'Healthy Cities' initiative 97
Housing Investment Plans (HIPs) 22
Hughes, Robert 119
hung authorities 22, 55–6, 58, 65–6

implementation (of strategic
initiatives) xii, 47, 129–30, 143
incrementalism ix, 109–11
information technology 99
INLOGOV 9
Institute for Operational Research 34
Islington LBC 88, 93

Kirklees MBC 118–19

Labour party 30, 46, 56, 57, 68, 101,
105
Leicestershire CC 68

Liberal Democrat party 56
Local Authorities Act 1933 30
Local Government Management
Board (LGMB) 11, 15–16
Local Government, Planning and
Land Act 1980 106
local government reorganisation
(1974) 9
Local Government Review 5, 19, 124

McGarvey, Neil 74, 76, 78, 87
management theory 32–5
manifestos (party) 56, 61
marketing (in local government) 6,
12, 77
Maud Committee (1967) 31, 34
Maud, Sir John 31
Merton, Robert 32
Midwinter, Aurthur 75, 76, 78, 87
Mintzberg, Henry 37–40
mission statements ix, xi, 1, 26, 71–85,
86, 87

National Forest 96
National Lottery grants 96, 97, 108
National Non-domestic Rate (NNDR)
46, 106
neighbourhood approach 20
New Forest DC 92
Norwich City Council 90

operational management 7, 37, 144
operations research 33–4
opposition parties (and strategy) 57,
62–3
'opting out' of schools (from LA
control) 19, 88
organisational capacity 124–36
organisational change 122–38
organisational context (or corporate
strategy) 42–53
organisational development 130–4

Parsons Talcolt 32
participation 77–8
partnership 11, 73, 77, 78, 79, 87
party politicisation (of local
    government) 30, 55–6
personal development plans 1–4
pilot schemes 137
Planning, Programmes and
    Budgetary Systems (PPB) 34, 35,
    110
Policing Plans 22
policy planning systems 31, 36
policy units 128–9, 136, 143
political context (of corporate
    strategy) 45, 47–8, 54–68, 109, 122
political leadership (in local
    government) 56–8, 68, 125
  relations with chief executive
    58–60, 68
Poll tax/community charge 106
priority-based budgeting 110–11,
    112–15
private sector (and strategy) xi, 1,
    5–6, 109
public involvement (in strategy) 14,
    138–9, 144
public service ethos 74, 77
purchaser/provider split 11

quality 76, 78, 79, 80, 83, 87, 115
quangos 32

Rate Support Grant (RSG) 46, 116
Redbridge LBC 73
Redcliffe-Maud Committee Report
    (1969) 37
'relative' strategies 19–20, 24
resource allocation processes 3, 7, 8,
    11, 13, 17, 22–3, 36, 42, 46, 48–9,
    55, 105–20, 136
role and purpose (of local
    government) 20–2

Sandwell MBC 113, 116–18, 138
Schultz, John x
service strategies 14–15, 22–3, 25,
    88–9, 102–4
Shropshire CC 74, 75
Single Regeneration Budget (SRB) 25,
    96, 106, 108, 130
Skelcher, Chris 82
soft strategy 40
Soterenta, M. 39–40
Southwark LBC 72
staffing implications (of corporate
    strategy) 49
Standard Spending Assessments
    (SSAs) 106, 113
Stewart, John 7, 9, 81
strategic champions 50, 55, 57, 67,
    126–9
strategic choice ix, x, xi, 17–18, 23
strategic effectiveness 48–50
strategic issues 1–4, 93–6
strategic management ix–x, 1, 5, 6, 18,
    24, 27, 41, 121–45
strategic monitoring 1
strategic planning x, xii, 1, 5, 6, 18,
    21–2, 24, 27, 36–40, 41, 45–8, 86,
    97–100, 134–6
strategic plans ix, x, 17–18, 134
strategic review 1, 51
strategic visions ix, xi, 24, 26, 86–104,
    135
strategy xi, 1
    see also corporate strategy
Structure Plans 22
Sunderland MBC 92
Sutton LBC 79, 138
systems theory 32–3

Tameside MBC 74
Tavistock Institute of Human
    Relations 34
Taylor, Frederick 32

Thatcher, Margaret 36
topic-based strategies 24, 25
'total strategy' 39
Tower Hamlets LBC 20
town clerk, role of 30, 31–2
traffic control 92
Training and Enterprise Councils
    (TECs) 106
Transportation Policy and Plans
    (TPPs) 22
trend analysis 97–101, 104

unitary development plans (UDPs) 22

Urban Development Corporations
    (UDCs) 106

Walsall MBC 74, 75
Warwickshire CC 66
Weber, Max 32
'wicked issues' 24, 91, 137
Wildavsky, Aaron 35
Wiltshire CC 92
Wolverhampton MBC 72, 90
Wyre DC 138, 141–2

zero-based budgeting 110,115